Modern Critical Interpretations

The Tales of Poe

Bloom's Modern Critical Interpretations

The Tales of Poe

Edited and with an introduction by

Harold Bloom
Sterling Professor of the Humanities
Yale University

Chelsea House Publishers
PHILADELPHIA

Printed and bound in the United States of America
20 19 18 17 16 15 14 13 12 11

∞ The paper used in this publication meets the minimum
requirements of the American National Standard for
Permanence of Paper for Printed Library Materials,
Z39.48-1984.

Library of Congress Cataloging-in-Publication Data
The Tales of Poe.
  (Modern critical interpretations)
  Bibliography: p.
  Includes index.
  Summary: A collection of critical essays on Poe's tales of
horror arranged in chronological order of publication.
  1. Poe, Edgar Allan, 1809–1849. Tales. 2. Horror tales,
American—History and criticism. [1. Poe, Edgar Allen,
1809–1849. Tales. 2. Horror stories—History and criticism. 3.
American literature—History and criticism] I. Bloom,
Harold. II. Series.
PS2618.T32T3 1987   813'.3   86-34307
ISBN 1-55546-011-9

Contents

Editor's Note

This book brings together a representative selection of the most useful criticism available upon the tales of Edgar Allan Poe. The critical essays are reprinted here in the chronological order of their original publication. I am grateful to Wendell Piez for his aid in editing this volume.

My introduction sets the tales, and particularly "Ligeia," in the total context, problematical and influential, of Poe's literary work. The chronological sequence of criticism begins with Robert L. Carringer's study of how Poe's centers of space threaten the protagonists of his stories. Barton Levi St. Armand, centering upon "The Fall of the House of Usher," shows how Poe's use of the Gothic mode replaced the Sublime by "a numinous, nameless dread."

"The Cask of Amontillado" is read by Walter Stepp as an instance of ironic doubling, while Brian M. Barbour relates Poe's tales to their author's ironic rejection of American tradition and society. In a deconstructive analysis, Gregory S. Jay translates several of the tales as parables of "textual intercourse," a fit reading of the relation between Poe and French intellectual tradition.

Examining Poe's images of death, Gerald Kennedy praises the tales as refusing to join in the evasion or denial of mortality. Ken Frieden ends this volume with an advanced exegesis of narrative monologue in Poe, which he finds to be a perpetual transgression of the customary limits of monologue.

Introduction

Valéry, in a letter to Gide, asserted that "Poe is the only impeccable writer. He was never mistaken." If this judgment startles an American reader, it is less remarkable than Baudelaire's habit of making his morning prayers to God and to Edgar Poe. If we add the devotion of Mallarmé to what he called his master Poe's "severe ideas," then we have some sense of the scandal of what might be called "French Poe," perhaps as much a Gallic mystification as "French Freud." French Poe is less bizarre than French Freud, but more puzzling, because its literary authority ought to be overwhelming, and yet vanishes utterly when confronted by what Poe actually wrote. Here is the second stanza of the impeccable writer's celebrated lyric, "For Annie":

> Sadly, I know
>   I am shorn of my strength,
> And no muscle I move
>   As I lie at full length—
> But no matter!—I feel
>   I am better at length.

Though of a badness not to be believed, this is by no means unrepresentative of Poe's verse. Aldous Huxley charitably supposed that Baudelaire, Mallarmé and Valéry simply had no ear for English, and so just could not hear Poe's palpable vulgarity. Nothing even in Poe's verse is so wickedly funny as Huxley's parody in which a grand Miltonic touchstone is transmuted into the mode of Poe's "Ulalume." First Milton, in *Paradise Lost,* 4.268–273:

> Not that fair field
> Of Enna, where Proserpine gathering flowers

Her self a fairer flower by gloomy Dis
Was gathered, which cost Ceres all that pain
To seek her through the world;

Next, Huxley's Poe:

It was noon in the fair field of Enna,
　　When Proserpina gathering flowers—
　　Herself the most fragrant of flowers,
Was gathered away to Gehenna
　　By the Prince of Plutonian powers;
Was borne down the windings of Brenner
　　To the gloom of his amorous bowers—
Down the tortuous highway of Brenner
　　To the God's agapemonous bowers.

What then did Baudelaire hear, what music of thought, when he read the actual Poe of "Ulalume"?

Here once, through an alley Titanic,
　　Of cypress, I roamed with my Soul—
　　Of cypress, with Psyche, my Soul.
These were days when my heart was volcanic
　　As the scoriac rivers that roll—
　　As the lavas that restlessly roll
Their sulphurous currents down Yaanek,
　　In the ultimate climes of the Pole—
That groan as they roll down Mount Yaanek,
　　In the realms of the Boreal Pole.

If this were Edward Lear, poet of "The Dong with the Luminous Nose" or "The Jumblies," one might not question Baudelaire and the other apostles of French Poe. But the hard-driven Poe did not set out to write nonsense verse. His desire was to be the American Coleridge or Byron or Shelley, and his poetry, at its rare best, echoes those High Romantic forerunners with some grace and a certain plangent urgency. Yet even "The City in the Sea" is a touch too close to Byron's "Darkness," while "Israfel" weakly revises Shelley's "To a Skylark." Nineteenth-century American poetry is considerably better than it is generally acknowledged to be. There are no other figures comparable to Whitman and Dickinson, but at least the following are clearly preferable to Poe, taking them chronologically:

Bryant, Emerson, Longfellow, Whittier, Jones Very, Thoreau, Melville, Timrod and Tuckerman. Poe scrambles for twelfth place with Sidney Lanier; if this judgment seems harsh, or too arithmetical, it is prompted by the continued French overvaluation of Poe as lyricist. No reader who cares deeply for the best poetry written in English can care greatly for Poe's verse. Huxley's accusation of vulgarity and bad taste is just: "To the most sensitive and high-souled man in the world we should find it hard to forgive, shall we say, the wearing of a diamond ring on every finger. Poe does the equivalent of this in his poetry; we notice the solecism and shudder."

II

Whatever his early ambitions, Poe wrote relatively little verse; there are scarcely a hundred pages of it in the remarkable new edition of his complete writings, in two substantial volumes, published by the Library of America. The bulk of his work is in tale-telling and criticism, with the exception of the problematic *Eureka: A Prose Poem,* a hundred-page cosmology that I take to be Poe's answer to Emerson's Transcendental manifesto, *Nature.* Certainly *Eureka* is more of a literary achievement than Poe's verse, while the popularity and influence of the shorter tales has been and remains immense. Whether either *Eureka* or the famous stories can survive authentic criticism is not clear, but nothing could remove the stories from the canon anyway. They are a permanent element in Western literary culture, even though they are best read when we are very young. Poe's criticism has mixed repute, but in fact has never been made fully available until the Library of America edition.

Poe's survival raises perpetually the issue as to whether literary merit and canonical status necessarily go together. I can think of no other American writer, down to this moment, at once so inevitable and so dubious. Mark Twain catalogued Fenimore Cooper's literary offenses, but all that he exuberantly listed are minor compared to Poe's. Allen Tate, proclaiming Poe "our cousin" in 1949, at the centenary of Poe's death, remarked, "He has several styles, and it is not possible to damn them all at once." Uncritical admirers of Poe should be asked to read his stories aloud (but only to themselves!). The association between the acting style of Vincent Price and the styles of Poe is alas not gratuitous, and indeed is an instance of deep crying out unto deep. Lest I be considered unfair by those devoted to Poe, I hasten to quote him at his strongest as a storyteller. Here is the opening paragraph of "William Wilson," a tale admired by Dostoyevski and still central to the great Western topos of the double:

Let me call myself, for the present, William Wilson. The fair page lying before me need not be sullied with my real appellation. This has already been too much an object for the scorn—for the horror—for the detestation of my race. To the uttermost regions of the globe have not indignant winds bruited its unparalleled infamy? Oh, outcast of all outcasts most abandoned!—to the earth art thou not forever dead? to its honors, to its flowers, to its golden aspirations?—and a cloud, dense, dismal, and limitless, does it not hang eternally between thy hopes and heaven?

This rhetoric, including the rhetorical questions, is British Gothic rather than German Gothic, Ossian or Monk Lewis rather than Tieck or E. T. A. Hoffmann. Its palpable squalors require no commentary. The critical question surely must be: how does "William Wilson" survive its bad writing? Poe's awful diction, whether here or in "The Fall of the House of Usher" or "The Purloined Letter," seems to demand the decent masking of a competent French translation. The tale somehow is stronger than its telling, which is to say that Poe's actual text does not matter. What survives, despite Poe's writing, are the psychological dynamics and mythic reverberations of his stories about William Wilson and Roderick Usher. Poe can only gain by a good translation, and scarcely loses if each reader fully retells the stories to another. C. S. Lewis, defending the fantasies of George Macdonald, formulated a curious principle that seems to me more applicable to Poe than to Macdonald:

> The texture of his writing as a whole is undistinguished, at times fumbling. . . . But this does not quite dispose of him even for the literary critic. What he does best is fantasy—fantasy that hovers between the allegorical and the mythopoeic. And this, in my opinion, he does better than any man. The critical problem with which we are confronted is whether this art—the art of mythmaking—is a species of the literary art. The objection to so classifying it is that the Myth does not essentially exist in words at all. We all agree that the story of Balder is a great myth, a thing of inexhaustible value. But of whose version—whose *words*—are we thinking when we say this?
>
> (*George Macdonald, An Anthology*)

Lewis replies that he is not thinking of anyone's words, but of a particular pattern of events. Of course that means Lewis is thinking of his own words. He goes so far as to remember when I first heard the story of Kafka's *Castle* related in conversation and afterwards read the book for myself. The reading added nothing. I had already received the myth, which was all that mattered.

Clearly mistaken about Kafka, Lewis was certainly correct about Macdonald's *Lilith,* and I think the insight is valid for Poe's stories. Myths matter because we prefer them in our own words, and so Poe's diction scarcely distracts us from our retelling, to ourselves, his bizarre myths. There is a dreadful universalism pervading Poe's weird tales. The Freudian reductions of Marie Bonaparte pioneered at converting Poe's universalism into the psychoanalytical universalism, but Poe is himself so reductive that the Freudian translations are in his case merely redundant. Poe authentically frightens children, and the fright can be a kind of trauma. I remember reading Poe's tales and Bram Stoker's *Dracula,* each for the first time, when I was about ten. *Dracula* I shrugged off (at least until I confronted Bela Lugosi murmuring: "I never drink—wine!") but Poe induced nasty and repetitious nightmares that linger even now. Myth may be only what the Polish aphorist Stanislaw Lec once called it, "gossip grown old," but then Poe would have to be called a very vivid gossip, though not often a very eloquent one.

III

Critics, even good ones, admire Poe's stories for some of the oddest of reasons. Poe, a true Southerner, abominated Emerson, plainly perceiving that Emerson (like Whitman, like Lincoln) was not a Christian, not a royalist, not a classicist. Self-reliance, the Emersonian answer to Original Sin, does not exist in the Poe cosmos, where you necessarily start out damned, doomed, and dismal. But I think Poe detested Emerson for some of the same reasons Hawthorne and Melville more subtly resented him, reasons that persist in the most distinguished living American writer, Robert Penn Warren, and in many current academic literary critics in our country. If you dislike Emerson, you probably will like Poe. Emerson fathered pragmatism; Poe fathered precisely nothing, which is the way he would have wanted it. Yvor Winters accused Poe of obscurantism, but that truthful indictment no more damages Poe than does tastelessness and tone deafness. Emerson, for better and for worse, was and is the mind of America, but Poe was and is our hysteria, our uncanny unanimity in our repressions. I certainly do not intend to mean by this that Poe was deeper than Emerson in any way whatsoever. Emerson cheerfully and consciously threw out the past. Critics tend to share Poe's easy historicism; perhaps without knowing it, they are gratified that every Poe story is, in too clear a sense, over even as it begins. We don't have to wait for Madeline Usher and the house to fall in upon poor Roderick; they have fallen in upon him already, before the narrator comes upon the place. Emerson exalted freedom, which he and Thoreau usefully called "wildness." No one in Poe is or can be free or wild, and some academic admirers of Poe truly like everything and everyone to be in bondage to a universal past. To begin is to be free, godlike and Emersonian-Adamic, or Jeffersonian. But for a writer to be free is bewildering and even maddening. What American writers and their exegetes half-unknowingly love in Poe is his more-than-Freudian oppressive and curiously original sense and sensation of overdetermination. Walter Pater once remarked that museums depressed him because they made him doubt that anyone ever had once been young. No one in a Poe story ever was young. As D. H. Lawrence angrily observed, everyone in Poe is a vampire—Poe himself in particular.

IV

Among Poe's tales, the near-exception to what I have been saying is the longest and most ambitious, *The Narrative of Arthur Gordon Pym*, just as the best of Poe's poems is the long prose-poem *Eureka*. Alas, even these works are somewhat overvalued, if only because Poe's critics understandably become excessively eager to see him vindicated. *Pym* is readable, but *Eureka* is extravagantly repetitious. Auden was quite taken with *Eureka*, but could remember very little of it in conversation, and one can doubt that he read it through, at least in English. Poe's most advanced critic is John T. Irwin, in his book *American Hieroglyphics*. Irwin rightly centers upon *Pym*, while defending *Eureka* as an "aesthetic cosmology" addressed to what in each of us Freud called the "bodily ego." Irwin is too shrewd to assert that Poe's performance in *Eureka* fulfills Poe's extraordinary intentions:

> What the poem *Eureka*, at once pre-Socratic and post-Newtonian, asserts is the truth of the feeling, the bodily intuition, that the diverse objects which the mind discovers in contemplating external nature form a unity, that they are all parts of one body which, if not infinite, is so gigantic as to be beyond both the spatial and temporal limits of human perception. In *Eureka*, then,

Poe presents us with the paradox of a "unified" macrocosmic body that is without a totalizing image—an alogical, intuitive belief whose "truth" rests upon Poe's sense that cosmologies and myths of origin are forms of internal geography that, under the guise of mapping the physical universe, map the universe of desire.

Irwin might be writing of Blake, or of other visionaries who have sought to map total forms of desire. What Irwin catches, by implication, is Poe's troubling anticipation of what is most difficult in Freud, the "frontier concepts" between mind and body, such as the bodily ego, the nonrepressive defense of introjection, and above all, the drives or instincts. Poe, not just in *Eureka* and in *Pym*, but throughout his tales and even in some of his verse, is peculiarly close to the Freudian speculation upon the bodily ego. Freud, in *The Ego and the Id* (1923), resorted to the uncanny language of E. T. A. Hoffmann (and of Poe) in describing this difficult notion:

The ego is first and foremost a bodily ego; it is not merely a surface entity, but is itself the projection of a surface. If we wish to find an anatomical analogy for it we can best identify it with the "cortical homunculus" of the anatomists, which stands on its head in the cortex, sticks up its heels, faces backwards and, as we know, has its speech-area on the left-hand side.

A footnote in the English translation of 1927, authorized by Freud but never added to the German editions, elucidates the first sentence of this description in a way analogous to the crucial metaphor in Poe that concludes *The Narrative of Arthur Gordon Pym*:

I.e. the ego is ultimately derived from bodily sensations, chiefly from those springing from the surface of the body, besides, as we have seen above, representing the superficies of the mental apparatus.

A considerable part of Poe's mythological power emanates from his own difficult sense that the ego is always a bodily ego. The characters of Poe's tales live out nearly every conceivable fantasy of introjection and identification, seeking to assuage their melancholia by psychically devouring the lost objects of their affections. D. H. Lawrence, in his *Studies in Classic American Literature* (1923), moralized powerfully against Poe, condemning him for "the will-to-love and the will-to-consciousness, asserted against death itself. The pride of human conceit in KNOWLEDGE." It is illuminating that Lawrence attacked Poe in much the same spirit as he attacked Freud, who is interpreted in *Psychoanalysis and the Unconscious* as somehow urging us to violate the taboo against incest. The interpretation is as extravagant as Lawrence's thesis that Poe urged vampirism upon us, but there remains something suggestive in Lawrence's violence against both Freud and Poe. Each placed the elitist individual in jeopardy, Lawrence implied, by hinting at the primacy of fantasy not just in the sexual life proper, but in the bodily ego's constitution of itself through acts of incorporation and identification.

The cosmology of *Eureka* and the narrative of *Pym* alike circle around fantasies of incorporation. *Eureka's* subtitle is "An Essay on the Material and Spiritual Universe" and what Poe calls its "general proposition" is heightened by italics: *"In the Original Unity of the First Thing lies the Secondary Cause of all Things, with the Germ of their Inevitable Annihilation."* Freud, in his cosmology, *Beyond the Pleasure Principle,* posited that the inorganic had preceded the organic, and also that it was the tendency of all things to return to their original state. Consequently, the aim of all life was death. The death drive, which became crucial for Freud's later dualisms, is nevertheless pure mythology, since Freud's only evidence for it was the repetition compulsion, and it is an extravagant leap from repetition to death. This reliance upon one's own mythology may have prompted Freud's audacity when, in the *New Introductory Lectures,* he admitted that the theory of drives was, so to speak, his own mythology, drives being not only magnificent conceptions but particularly sublime in their indefiniteness. I wish I could assert that *Eureka* has some of the speculative force of *Beyond the Pleasure Principle* or even of Freud's disciple Ferenczi's startling *Thalassa: A Theory of Genitality;* but *Eureka* does badly enough when compared to Emerson's *Nature,* which itself has only a few passages worthy of what Emerson wrote afterwards. And yet Valéry in one sense was justified in his praise for *Eureka.* For certain intellectuals, *Eureka* performs a mythological function akin to what Poe's tales continue to do for hosts of readers. *Eureka* is unevenly written, badly repetitious, and sometimes opaque in its abstractness, but like the tales it seems not to have been composed by a particular individual. The universalism of a common nightmare informs it. If the tales lose little, or even gain, when we retell them to others in our own words, *Eureka* gains by Valéry's observations, or by the summaries of recent critics like John Irwin or Daniel Hoffman. Translation even into his own language always benefits Poe.

I haven't the space, or the desire, to summarize *Eureka,* and no summary is likely to do anything besides deadening both my readers and myself. Certainly Poe was never more passionately sincere than in composing *Eureka*, of which he affirmed: *"What I here propound is true."* But these are the closing sentences of *Eureka:*

> Think that the sense of individual identity will be gradually merged in the general consciousness—that Man, for example, ceasing imperceptibly to feel himself Man, will at length attain that awfully triumphant epoch when he shall recognize his existence as that of Jehovah. In the meantime bear in mind that all is Life—Life—Life within Life—the less within the greater, and all within the *Spirit Divine.*

To this, Poe appends a "Note":

> The pain of the consideration that we shall lose our individual identity, ceases at once when we further reflect that the process, as above described, is, neither more nor less than that of the absorption, by each individual intelligence of all other intelligences (that is, of the Universe) into its own. That God may be all in all, *each* must become God.

Allen Tate, not unsympathetic to his cousin, Mr. Poe, remarked of Poe's extinction in *Eureka* that "there is a lurid sublimity in the spectacle of his taking God along with him into a grave which is not smaller than the universe." If we read closely, Poe's trope is "absorption," and we are where we always are in Poe, amid ultimate fantasies of introjection in which the bodily ego and the cosmos become indistinguishable. Again, I suspect this judgment hardly weakens Poe, since his strength is no more cognitive than it is stylistic. Poe's mythology, like the mythology of psychoanalysis that we cannot yet bear to acknowledge as primarily a mythology, is peculiarly appropriate to any modernism, whether you want to call it early, high or post-modernism. The definitive judgment belongs here to T. W. Adorno, certainly the most authentic theoretician of all modernisms, in his last book, *Aesthetic Theory.* Writing on "reconciliation and mimetic adaptation to death," Adorno blends the insights of Jewish negative theology and psychoanalysis:

> Whether negativity is the barrier or the truth of art is not for art to decide. Art works are negative *per se* because they are subject to the law of objectification; that is, they kill what they objectify, tearing it away from its context of immediacy and real

life. They survive because they bring death. This is particularly true of modern art, where we notice a general mimetic abandonment to reification, which is the principle of death. Illusion in art is the attempt to escape from this principle. Baudelaire marks a watershed, in that art after him seeks to discard illusion without resigning itself to being a thing among things. The harbingers of modernism, Poe and Baudelaire, were the first technocrats of art.

Baudelaire was more than a technocrat of art, as Adorno knew, but Poe would be only that except for his mythmaking gift. C. S. Lewis may have been right when he insisted that such a gift could exist even apart from other literary endowments. Blake and Freud are inescapable mythmakers who were also cognitively and stylistically powerful. Poe is a great fantasist whose thoughts were commonplace and whose metaphors were dead. Fantasy, mythologically considered, combines the stances of Narcissus and Prometheus, which are ideologically antithetical to one another, but figuratively quite compatible. Poe is at once the Narcissus and the Prometheus of his nation. If that is right, then he is inescapable, even though his tales contrast weakly with Hawthorne's, his poems scarcely bear reading, and his speculative discourses fade away in juxtaposition to Emerson's, his despised Northern rival.

V

To define Poe's mythopoeic inevitability more closely, I turn to his story "Ligeia" and to the end of *Pym*. Ligeia, a tall, dark, slender transcendentalist, dies murmuring a protest against the feeble human will, which cannot keep us forever alive. Her distraught and nameless widower, the narrator, endeavors to comfort himself, first with opium, and then with a second bride, "the fair-haired and blue-eyed Lady Rowena Trevanian, of Tremaine." Unfortunately, he has little use for this replacement, and so she sickens rapidly and dies. Recurrently, the corpse revivifies, only to die yet again and again. At last, the cerements are stripped away, and the narrator confronts the undead Ligeia, attired in the death-draperies of her now evaporated successor.

As a parable of the vampiric will, this works well enough. The learned Ligeia presumably has completed her training in the will during her absence, or perhaps merely owes death a substitute, the insufficiently transcendental Rowena. What is mythopoeically more impressive is the ambiguous question of the narrator's will. Poe's own life, like Walt Whitman's, is an American mythology, and what all of us generally remember about it is that Poe married his first cousin, Virginia Clemm, before she turned fourteen. She died a little more than ten years later, having been a semi-invalid for most of that time. Poe himself died less than three years after her, when he was just forty. "Ligeia," regarded by Poe as his best tale, was written a bit more than a year into the marriage. The later Freud implicitly speculates that there are no accidents; we die because we will to die, our character being also our fate. In Poe's myth also, ethos is the daemon, and the daemon is our destiny. The year after Virginia died, Poe proposed marriage to the widowed poet Sarah Helen Whitman. Biographers tell us that the lady's doubts were caused by rumors of Poe's bad character, but perhaps Mrs. Whitman had read "Ligeia"! In any event, this marriage did not take place, nor did Poe survive to marry another widow, his childhood sweetheart Elmira Royster Shelton. Perhaps she too might have read "Ligeia" and forborne.

The narrator of "Ligeia" has a singularly bad memory, or else a very curious relationship to his own will, since he begins by telling us that he married Ligeia without ever having troubled to learn her family name. Her name itself is legend, or romance, and that was enough. As the story's second paragraph hints, the lady was an opium dream with the footfall of a shadow. The implication may be that there never was such a lady, or even that if you wish to incarnate your reveries, then you must immolate your consubstantial Rowena. What is a touch alarming to the narrator is the intensity of Ligeia's passion for him, which was manifested however only by glances and voice so long as the ideal lady lived. Perhaps this baffled intensity is what kills Ligeia, through a kind of narcissistic dialectic, since she is dominated not by the will of her lust but by the lust of her will. She wills her infinite passion towards the necessarily inadequate narrator and when (by implication) he fails her, she turns the passion of her will against dying and at last against death. Her dreadful poem, "The Conqueror Worm," prophesies her cyclic return from death: "Through a circle that ever returneth in / To the self-same spot." But when she does return, the spot is hardly the same. Poor Rowena only becomes even slightly interesting to her narrator-husband when she sickens unto death, and her body is wholly usurped by the revived Ligeia. And yet the wretched narrator is a touch different, if only because his narcissism is finally out of balance with his first wife's grisly Prometheanism. There are no final declarations of Ligeia's passion as the story concludes. The triumph of her will is complete, but we know that the narrator's will has not blent itself into Ligeia's. His renewed obsession with her eyes testifies to a continued sense of her dae-monic power over him, but his final words hint at what the story's opening confirms: she will not be back for long—and remains "my lost love."

The conclusion of *Pym* has been brilliantly analyzed by John Irwin, and so I want to glance only briefly at what is certainly Poe's most effective closure:

> And now we rushed into the embraces of the cataract, where a chasm threw itself open to receive us. But there arose in our pathway a shrouded human figure, very far larger in its pro-portions than any dweller among men. And the hue of the skin of the figure was of the perfect whiteness of the snow.

Irwin demonstrates Poe's reliance here upon the Romantic topos of the Alpine White Shadow, the magnified projection of the observer himself. The chasm Pym enters is the familiar Romantic Abyss, not a part of the natural world but belonging to eternity, before the creation. Reflected in that abyss, Pym beholds his own shrouded form, perfect in the whiteness of the natural context. Presumably, this is the original bodily ego, the Gnostic self before the fall into creation. As at the close of *Eureka,* Poe brings Alpha and Omega together in an apocalyptic circle. I suggest we read Pym's, which is to say Poe's, white shadow as the American triumph of the will, as illusory as Ligeia's usurpation of Rowena's corpse.

Poe teaches us, through Pym and Ligeia, that as Americans we are both subject and object to our own quests. Emerson, in Americanizing the European sense of the abyss, kept the self and the abyss separate as facts: "There may be two or three or four steps, according to the genius of each, but for every seeing soul there are two absorbing facts—I and the Abyss." Poe, seeking to avoid Emersonianism, ends with only one fact, and it is more a wish than a fact: "I will to be the Abyss." This metaphysical despair has appealed to the Southern American literary tradition and to its Northern followers. The appeal cannot be refuted, because it is myth, and Poe backed the myth with his life as well as his work. If the Northern or Emersonian myth of our literary culture culminates in the beautiful image of Walt Whitman as wound-dresser, moving as a mothering father through the Civil War Washington, D.C., hospitals, then the Southern or countermyth achieves its perfect stasis at its start, with Poe's snow-white shadow shroud-ing the chasm down which the boat of the soul is about to plunge. Poe's genius was for negativity and opposition, and the affirmative force of Emer-sonian America gave him the impetus his daemonic will required.

VI

It would be a relief to say that Poe's achievement as a critic is not mythological, but the splendid, new and almost complete edition of his essays, reviews and marginalia testifies otherwise. It shows Poe indeed to have been Adorno's "technocrat of art." Auden defended Poe's criticism by contrasting the subjects Baudelaire was granted—Delacroix, Constantin Guys, Wagner—with the books Poe was given to review, such as *The Christian Florist, The History of Texas,* and *Poetical Remains of the Late Lucretia Maria Davidson.* The answer to Auden is that Poe also wrote about Bryant, Byron, Coleridge, Dickens, Hawthorne, Washington Irving, Longfellow, Shelley, and Tennyson; a ninefold providing scope enough for any authentic critical consciousness. Nothing that Poe had to say about these poets and storytellers is in any way memorable or at all an aid to reading them. There are no critical insights, no original perceptions, no accurate or illuminating juxtapositions or historical placements. Here is Poe on Tennyson, from his *Marginalia,* which generally surpasses his other criticism:

> Why do some persons fatigue themselves in attempts to unravel such phantasy-pieces as the "Lady of Shalott"? . . . If the author did not deliberately propose to himself a suggestive indefinitiveness of meaning, with the view of bringing about a definitiveness of vague and therefore of spiritual *effect*—this, at least, arose from the silent analytical promptings of that poetic genius which, in its supreme development, embodies all orders of intellectual capacity.

I take this as being representative of Poe's criticism, because it is uninterestingly just plain *wrong* about "The Lady of Shalott." No other poem, even by the great word-painter Tennyson, is deliberately so definite in meaning and effect. Everything vague precisely is excluded in this perhaps most Pre-Raphaelite of all poems, where each detail contributes to an impression that might be called hard-edged phantasmagoria. If we take as the three possibilities of nineteenth-century practical criticism the sequence of Arnold, Pater, and Wilde, we find Poe useless in all three modes: Arnold's seeing the object as in itself it really is, Pater's seeing accurately one's own impression of the object, and the divine Oscar's sublime seeing of the object as in itself it really is not. If "The Lady of Shalott" is the object, then Poe does not see anything: the poem as in itself it is, one's impression of the poem as that is, or best of all the Wildean sense of what is missing or excluded from the poem. Poe's descriptive terms are "indefinitiveness" and "vague," but Tennyson's poem is just the reverse:

> She left the web, she left the loom,
> She made three paces through the room,
> She saw the water-lily bloom,
> She saw the helmet and the plume,
>   She looked down to Camelot.
> Out flew the web and floated wide;
> The mirror cracked from side to side;
> "The curse is come upon me," cried
>   The Lady of Shalott.

No, Poe as practical critic is a true match for most of his contemporary subjects, such as S. Anna Lewis, author of *The Child of the Sea and Other Poems* (1848). Of her lyric "The Forsaken," Poe wrote, "We have read this little poem more than twenty times and always with increasing admiration. *It is inexpressibly beautiful*" (Poe's italics). I quote only the first of its six stanzas:

> It hath been said—for all who die
>   there is a tear;
> Some pining, bleeding heart to sigh
>   O'er every bier:
> But in that hour of pain and dread
>   Who will draw near
> Around my humble couch and shed
>   One farewell tear?

Well, but there is Poe as theoretician, Valéry has told us. Acute self-consciousness in Poe was strongly misread by Valéry as the inauguration and development of severe and skeptical ideas. Presumably, this is the Poe of three famous essays: "The Philosophy of Composition," "The Rationale of Verse," and "The Poetic Principle." Having just reread these pieces, I have no possibility of understanding a letter of Valéry to Mallarmé which prizes the theories of Poe as being "so profound and so insidiously learned." Certainly we prize the theories of Valéry for just those qualities, and so I have come full circle to where I began, with the mystery of French Poe. Valéry may be said to have read Poe in the critical modes both of Pater and of Wilde. He saw his impression of Poe clearly, and he saw Poe's essays as in themselves they really were not. Admirable, and so Valéry brought to culmination the critical myth that is French Poe.

VII

Whose head is swinging from the swollen strap?
Whose body smokes along the bitten rails,
Bursts from a smoldering bundle far behind
In back forks of the chasms of the brain—
Puffs from a riven stump far out behind
In interborough fissures of the mind . . .?

Hart Crane's vision of Poe, in the "Tunnel" section of *The Bridge,* tells us again why the mythopoeic Poe is inescapable for American literary mythology. Poe's nightmare projections and introjections suggest the New York City subway as the new underground, where Coleridge's "deep Romantic chasm" has been internalized into "the chasms of the brain." Whatever his actual failures as poet and critic, whatever the gap between style and idea in his tales, Poe is central to the American canon, both for us and for the rest of the world. Hawthorne implicitly and Melville explicitly made far more powerful critiques of the Emersonian national hope, but they were by no means wholly negative in regard to Emerson and his pragmatic vision of American Self-Reliance. Poe was savage in denouncing minor transcendentalists like Bronson Alcott and William Ellery Channing, but his explicit rejection of Emerson confined itself to the untruthful observation that Emerson was indistinguishable from Thomas Carlyle. Poe should have survived to read Carlyle's insane and amazing pamphlet "The Nigger Question," which he would have adored. Mythologically, Poe is necessary because all of his work is a hymn to negativity. Emerson was a great theoretician of literature as of life, a good practical critic (when he wanted to be, which was not often), a very good poet (sometimes) and always a major aphorist and essayist. Poe, on a line-by-line or sentence-by-sentence basis, is hardly a worthy opponent. But looking in the French way, as T. S. Eliot recommended, "we see a mass of unique shape and impressive size to which the eye constantly returns." Eliot was probably right, in mythopoeic terms.

Poe's Tales: The Circumscription of Space

Robert L. Carringer

Poe's stature as a writer of fiction is based principally upon about fifteen items: a small collection of detective stories (written in the first half of the 1840s) and about a dozen of those bizarre and morbid romances he called "arabesques" (all but two, "MS. Found in a Bottle" and "The Cask of Amontillado," written between 1835 and 1843). The peculiar nature of the dilemma *Pym* got Poe into becomes clear when one examines a dominant pattern of experience in these major tales. "The prevailing invitation of Poe's narrators," Terence Martin reminds us, "is for us to witness an act or process of destruction." In every one of the major arabesques an act or process of destruction is central to the plot: plague and bloody red death in "The Masque of the Red Death"; the illness and death of a woman in "Morella," "Ligeia," and "Eleonora," and of twins in "The Fall of the House of Usher"; the prospect of violent death brought about by powerful external forces in "MS. Found in a Bottle," "A Descent into the Maelström," and "The Pit and the Pendulum"; and murderous attacks on others, which entail self-destructive consequences, in "Berenice," "William Wilson," "The Tell-Tale Heart," "The Black Cat," and "The Cask of Amontillado." There are other features that give this material a kind of fundamental sameness despite the variety of motifs and situations. Most of Poe's best writing (all but "The Masque of the Red Death" in the above group) is in the form of first-person narratives. Often there are specific incidents or details that link the narrator with the author. Characteristically,

From *PMLA* 89, no. 3 (May 1974). © 1974 by the Modern Language Association of America.

Poe's protagonists exhibit a morbid preoccupation with various forms of physical disintegration (especially decay and putrefaction), and Poe has an almost clinical regard for the representation of mental excitement, especially those forms of terror that are aroused by the prospect of death or derangement for his narrators. His imaginative commitment, as D. H. Lawrence remarked many years ago, is to "the disintegration processes of his own psyche."

There is abundant evidence, in Quinn's biography and elsewhere, that Poe was almost compulsively masochistic. Awareness of such details, however, has led more often to speculative psychology than to literary criticism, but recently there have been attempts to view Poe's destructiveness in terms other than those of neurotic personality.

Richard Wilbur argues in an extremely influential essay that Poe's destructiveness is, paradoxically, a fundamentally creative impulse whose aim is to obliterate earthly experience in what Poe called "a wild effort to reach the Beauty above." According to Wilbur, this otherworldly impulse signifies the yearning of a divided nature to be whole again, a conflict that is finally objectified into the cosmic scheme of *Eureka,* Poe's late prose poem on the final reunification of matter and spirit in the universe. In his chapter on Poe in *The Design of the Present* John Lynen also argues that a longing for a spiritual ideal of beauty underlies Poe's destructiveness, though Lynen holds that it should be understood literally, not as an allegory on psychological states. Destructiveness in Poe, he believes, is a calculated strategy of indirection, of "expressing things through their opposites"—beauty through the grotesque, rebirth in a higher consciousness through a (necessary) dying in this one.

This line of argumentation rests on several assumptions: that Poe's questing after what he calls ideal beauty should be taken entirely seriously; that this quest, which is the stated intention of his poetry, is the underlying motive of his fiction as well; that this quest anticipates the theme of ultimate reunification of matter and spirit in the universe, which receives mature expression in *Eureka*; and that *Eureka* is the philosophical key to all of Poe's serious work. This entire structure of assumptions can be called into serious question. Despite the important studies of *Eureka* by Davidson and others, it is still respectable to hold that this work can be seen in somewhat the same light as "The Philosophy of Composition," another after-the-fact attempt at pseudoscientific system-building designed to explain certain obsessive peculiarities in their creator's imaginative work. Important studies from *The Histrionic Mr. Poe* to Terence Martin's have testified to Poe's "posing" and his incurable love of playing games. There is as much reason to regard the quest for ideal beauty as a pose as there is to regard it as anything else. Moreover, his use of wan and ghoulish maidens and putrefying corpses as earthly symbols of spiritual beauty has all the makings of a typical Poe joke. There *is* a strong yearning for unattainable feminine figures on the part of some Poe protagonists. It is especially strong in the early poetry and in those early tales such as "Berenice," "Morella," and "Ligeia" in which a male protagonist longs to be reunited with a lost wife or lover. Around 1839, however, the need that this motif represented appears to have been significantly modified or fulfilled (or perhaps he merely tired of it); for after Roderick Usher collapses into death in his dead sister's embrace, the impulse ceases to provide the stimulus for Poe's best work. Thereafter, it appears most characteristically in prosaic, otherworldly dialogues between abstract masculine and feminine figures, and when the earlier motif reappears it is significantly modified, as in "Eleonora," in which the bereaved lover returns to the world and takes another woman with Eleonora's blessing, bestowed from beyond the grave. "William Wilson" (published next after "Usher"), Poe's definitive alter-ego narrative, initiates a new phase in the fiction; and for several years Poe's most interesting narratives (discounting the detective stories) involve a first-person protagonist in some form of self-encounter. As a matter of fact, almost simultaneously with the publication of one of the best of these, "The Pit and the Pendulum," he explicitly renounced the "idea of the Beautiful" as a legitimate province of the tale, and held that verisimilar presentation of ratiocination, terror, passion, or horror is a more suitable interest for a writer of short fiction. One could argue that Poe's supreme achievement in fiction is a series of stories based on this formula written from 1839 to 1843 which depict first-person narrators discovering their capacity for violent, irrational behavior. As Harry Levin and others have pointed out, his chief contribution to fiction is a technique for effectively portraying the impact of those discoveries on consciousness, and I suspect that the chief value of the tales for most readers is as highly realistic, technically sophisticated allegories on the consequences of self-destructive impulses.

Besides physical disintegration and psychological terror, we may note as a third identifying characteristic of a story by Poe a strong impulse to delimit space. Indeed, as we shall see, there is a way in which this third characteristic can be used as a means to explain the other two. Few readers can have failed to notice that most of the time in most of the stories the Poe protagonist is conspicuously *within* something. In six of the thirteen tales previously named, the principal activity takes place within a single room, and within a series of rooms in two others. Tombs figure prominently in four, secret compartments in three others. Even outdoors activity (which is uncommon) is very carefully framed (as in "Eleonora") by natural limits such as hillsides, steep cliffs, or overhanging foliage. Most key moments of action in Poe conspicuously involve severely restrictive enclosures, from stuffy Gothic rooms to deep, dark pits to damp, musty caves to whirlpools, coffins, tombs, and various kinds of secret recesses within a wall or underneath a floor. Poe was very much aware of the persistence of this trait, and in "The Philosophy of Composition" he tried to account for it by explaining that "a close *circumscription of space* is absolutely necessary to the effect of the insulated incident." That is, in terms of his theory of fiction, a tale must have an absolute consistency of tone and atmosphere in order for it to achieve a unified effect; a circumscribed setting is part of this overall economy of form. But Richard Wilbur points to a curious paradox in "William Wilson." During the course of the story Wilson makes his way from Stoke Newington to Eton, from Eton to Oxford, and then to Rome by way of Paris, Vienna, Berlin, Moscow, Naples, and Egypt. "And yet for all his travels," Mr. Wilbur observes, "Wilson never seems to set foot out-of-doors." This paradox occurs even more tellingly in tales involving actual movement in space. In both "MS. Found in a Bottle" and "A Descent into the Maelström," in a reversal of all conventional associations, Poe manages to have his narrator delimited by space *on the ocean.* Poe's comment may be a perfectly valid esthetic observation for those stories to which it applies, but clearly the persistence of the motif into other situations suggests the appropriateness of alternative explanations.

According to Wilbur, Poe's withdrawals are a typical Romantic allegory on the artistic process and circumscription symbolizes "the isolation of the poetic soul in visionary reverie or trance." "When we find one of Poe's characters in a remote valley, or a claustral room," Mr. Wilbur continues, "we know that he is in the process of dreaming his way out of the world." But the worlds into which Poe's protagonists dream their way are fraught with their own special dangers and threats. Prominent among the dangers is one that confronts several protagonists at their moments of truth. One lies at the bottom of a dark pit and is about to be crushed to death by its closing walls. Another moves through the diminishing space of seven rooms to a final confrontation with bloody death in the seventh. Still another is lured through the diminishing space of a cave and bricked up at last in a narrow recess in the wall. We should note, first, that to circumscribe a Poe character is usually to involve him in some form of violent destructiveness. Clearly, then, circumscription is somehow intimately bound up with that penchant for disaster that characterizes the typical

Poe protagonist. As the preceding examples indicate, it is not circumscription alone that is most important but rather what that state signifies, the possibility of being further circumscribed, that is, the threat of being confronted with diminishing space. This is what lies behind that curious paradox in the sea "voyages." In both of them Poe finds a pretext that allows him to reverse all conventional associations that hold the sea to be a place of infinite expanse, and in each one at the climax has his narrator being borne along diminishing concentric circles toward violent death. The major terms of this formula (circumscription involves destruction) appear in other guises. For instance, two 1843 masterpieces, "The Tell-Tale Heart" and "The Black Cat," both involve a secret crime of the narrator's, the evidence of which is buried away in a narrow enclosure. Both narrator-protagonists are irresistibly drawn back to their secret hiding places, and the same irrational impulse compels them to reveal their crimes and thereby open the path to their own destruction. As in the sea and pit narratives, destiny for the narrator-protagonist is a crucial encounter with diminished space. Wilbur reaches his conclusion by dealing primarily with those narratives like "Berenice," "Ligeia," and "The Fall of the House of Usher" which are set principally in the narrator-protagonist's ornate private chamber; but we should recognize how space is unstable even in these. Poe's rooms in these stories, as Mr. Wilbur notes, are usually very prominently enclosures within enclosures. But in all three the narrator's compelling motive is to be further circumscribed. He has suffered a loss of his beloved and will be whole again only after his earthly identity has been destroyed and he has been reunited with what is shut away in the tomb.

If Poe's protagonists exhibited a morbid fear of enclosures, one could label it a sign of claustrophobia and leave it at that. But it is not space itself that threatens. Rather, it is some unknown and irresistible thing that lurks at the point where space ends. One is faced, therefore, with a key question: What is at the center of diminishing space?

Among the characteristic forms that appear at Poe's centers are girls in coffins, murdered victims, and natural images of destruction (such as whirlpools). Again, there is diversity, but there is also a way to see an underlying consistency among these different forms. The clue is provided, I think, by "William Wilson," perhaps the single most important Poe story for an understanding of the sources of his fiction in his life. The central conflict in "William Wilson" is between moral and premoral aspects of being; the second William Wilson is the objectified conscience of the libertine first Wilson. In the story, moral being is threatened and finally destroyed by the unchecked impulses of its dissolute counterpart. Specifically, sexuality proves to be the last straw: the second Wilson appears just after the first has admitted to having sexual designs on the young wife of an aged Duke, and his appearance sends his counterpart into a murderous rage. Sexuality is a frequent threat for Poe protagonists: Poe's most productive period begins with a narrative involving a disguised bloody act of desexualization, the pulling of Berenice's *vaginae dentes*, and in the various sequels earthly women are safely shut away in tombs while a lover yearns for cold, sexless "ideal" women. His last major story, "The Cask of Amontillado"— set, significantly, like the climax of "William Wilson," in carnival (carnal?) times—progresses atypically to entrapment rather than disclosure and ends with the protagonist's libertine alter ego safely buried away (forever?) in a secret recess deep in the bowels of a cave. One might argue convincingly that "threat of sexuality" is really Poe's central theme, and that "the idea of the Beautiful" is merely one form of sublimation. But over-simplification of this sort is a disservice that has been rendered to Poe all too frequently. In "The Man of the Crowd," which followed shortly after "William Wilson," the libertine alter ego is presented as a kind of archetype of criminality. It is better to say more generally that the central conflict facing many of Poe's artist-surrogates is the one dramatized in the two narratives considered together: a conflict between two aspects of their own natures, their rational and moral selves versus the source of their capacity for "criminality" and destructive violence, their premoral natures. Other kinds of plots can be seen as variants on this conflict. For instance, the two sea "voyages" are metaphorically descents from rationality and order down into an inner source of destructive primal energies, symbolized by the boiling eye of a whirlpool. To drop a capital letter to lower case is to reveal an underlying metaphor in the death-of-women narratives: the yearning for "Psyche, my Soul" is a yearning for presexual psychic harmony; the obligatory entombment of earthly women in these narratives is a way of suppressing primal (sexual) energies. The conflict between contending facets of the self is often at the base of narratives involving murdered victims. Two of the best of these, "The Tell-Tale Heart" and "The Black Cat," resolve themselves in terms of an implied play on words. In both stories, the narrator, in a paranoid frenzy, destroys the threatening eye of an innocent antagonist. Later, an irrational impulse drives him to uncover the crime. There in the secret place is the victim but not the offensive organ. The progression of the story is implied by the pun: that which the narrator destroyed, an "Evil Eye," an objective fact, becomes the means of his own undoing, the subjective condition that it symbolizes, an "evil I." As in "William Wilson" a destructive act redounds upon its perpetrator with equally self-destructive force.

Why is it, Howard P. Vincent asks in *The Trying Out of "Moby-Dick,"* that "so many of the world's literary masterpieces have been studies of travel?" "The answer," he replies, "lies in the nature of the basic metaphor, common to all of them, of the voyage as a symbol of spiritual forthfaring: that even as the physical soul seeks new sights in strange places so the human soul in its necessary process of growth goes out into the sea of life. The fundamental metaphor of the voyage applies to Romantic allegories of withdrawal into self as well as to accounts of actual voyages. Just as unlimited expanses of ocean, prairie, or wilderness suggest an "area of total possibility" for the young American Adam, Poe's enclosures suggest his fictional universe of negative possibility and the severely restricted prospects and interests of his protagonists. By the same token, his centers of space are physically threatening to his protagonists because the internal condition that they symbolize is also threatening to the protagonist's rational and moral nature. For there, at the center of space toward which the protagonists of "Berenice," "A Descent into the Maelström," and "The Tell-Tale Heart" are driven, is an image of a thing that is also an image of themselves.

The "Mysteries" of Edgar Poe: The Quest for a Monomyth in Gothic Literature

Barton Levi St. Armand

In exploring the mysteries of Gothic taste, it is easy for the critic to forget that the whole genre was, first and foremost, a fashion, a style, and a mode of interior decoration. That the particular interior being redecorated was human consciousness itself is ancillary to the nature of Gothic as primarily an aesthetic revival which somehow managed to provide Romanticism with its first full set of swaddling clothes. The remarkable thing about this taste is that we can chart its serpentine course almost from work to work in terms of the development of theme, character, and popularity of novel modes and means of decoration. The Wandering Jew, who plays only a minor walk-on part in Lewis's *The Monk,* for example, emerges as the main character type of Maturin's *Melmoth.* Mrs. Radcliffe's Appenines somehow contribute both to Shelley's "Mont Blanc" and to the frozen Arctic landscapes of his wife's *Frankenstein.* The Venetian segment of *The Mysteries of Udolpho* becomes the whole focus of a tale like Poe's deliberately Byronic "The Assignation"; we cannot fully understand the rationale of its conclusion or the presence of "the cracked and blackened goblet" clutched in the marble hand of Poe's dead voluptuary unless we know that Radcliffe's hero-villain Montoni avoided death by using a special type of Venetian glass which splintered and bubbled when poison was poured into it. In such ways, both major and minor, one can chart the growth of Gothic romance from the first appearance of the species in the *Otranto* of 1764 to such late examples as Faulkner's *Absalom, Absalom!*

From *The Gothic Imagination: Essays in Dark Romanticism,* edited by G. R. Thompson. © 1974 by the President and Regents of Washington State University. Washington State University Press, 1974.

Yet, even considering Gothicism as a particular formal structure or burgeoning type, the extreme left-wing or avant-garde of Romanticism, with a curious organic vitality seemingly built into it, certain problems arise. These problems are those continuing ones of device and depth, control and connotation, adaptability and meaning. A mode can evolve so fast that, in an attempt to utilize the best of what the recent past has been as well as what the present is still yearning to be, it reaches a point of critical mass which collapses from within and leaves only an empty eclecticism. In the case of the Gothic genre, in all its manifestations—architectural and social as well as literary—this circumstance becomes doubly true. For the Gothic was an alien revival which took root in an age devoted to one supreme mode—that of Classicism, with its fidelity to decorum, uniformity, and the rule of law. To preserve its vitality, the Gothic always needed some new exotic quality, some as-yet-untapped antiquarian element, to grow and to flourish. Hence its frank sensationalism, its fantastic "outreaching comprehensiveness of sweep," to quote the American Gothicist, Herman Melville. The Gothic was nothing if not new and varied; yet at the same time, there was an unexpected mental growth as well, a dimensional growth in acuity of intelligence and refinement of consciousness. The problem was to impose or synthesize a style which would control, deepen, and extend the mode's previous line of development. In specific literary terms, it was the same process which led William Blake to purify the experimental chaos of the *Poetical Sketches* by utilizing the ingenuous hymns of Dr. Watts and so produce at last the *Songs of Innocence* and the *Songs of Experience*. Later, Blake was similarly to transmute the pseudo-Celtic meters of James Macpherson's *Ossian* (1762) into the bardic thunder of the *Prophetic Books*, proving that the mode, the style, the species bred in the unlikeliest places and consorted with the most disreputable models in order to bring forth a superior type.

In our own century, William Butler Yeats, emerging from that same Celtic twilight and its peculiar conjunctions of primal myth and Romantic fustian, of Blake and Macpherson, was to speak of "masterful images" that grew out of pure mind yet began in a "mound of refuse or the sweepings of a street." What remains important, however, is the fact that the Celtic and the Druidical were both manifestations of the taste for barbaric revivals which was to become known generally as "Gothic." The variety and adaptability of the style, from William Beckford's Oriental Gothic in *Vathek* to Herman Melville's remarkable cetological subspecies in *Moby-Dick*, masked an underlying search for a monomyth which could exploit the possibilities of this fanciful interior decoration while it unified Romantic multiplicity and became at the same time a paradigm for expressing fundamental human experience. The nature of this experience was in most cases (surprisingly enough given the Gothic's stiff anticlerical and anti-Catholic bias) profoundly inward, even "religious" in the broadest sense. It may have begun in Walpole's antiquarian fascination with a lost world of medieval superstition as a means of relieving the boredom of eighteenth-century social realities, but the religious impulse in Gothicism soon galloped from a concern with talking pictures and bleeding nuns to a consideration of man's position in a terrifying and inscrutable universe, an obsession with individual destiny and damnation, and a determined exploration of the mysteries of the soul itself.

"Mystery" is a word which we automatically associate with the Gothic genre since it found its way over and over again into so many Gothic titles, the most famous, of course, being *The Mysteries of Udolpho* (1794) by Ann Radcliffe. But the dimensions of the idea of Gothic mystery can lead us into a consideration of just what the control of the genre by an underlying monomyth entails. At the primary level, for example, the "mysteries" of Udolpho are common detective-story mysteries involving the solution of a contrived puzzle: what was the hideous thing behind the black veil which caused the sensitive Emily to swoon so plaintively and so frequently during her incarceration within the dark battlements of Udolpho? It was, we discover at the end of this monumental romance, only a medieval remnant of monkish superstition, a waxen votary object left as a penance by a long-vanished ancestor of the House of Udolpho. Yet Emily's timid lifting of the black veil has much deeper psychic resonances when, in later Romantic fiction, that veil becomes the Veil of Isis which, as Esther Harding explains, is also "the ever-changing form of nature, whose beauty and tragedy veil the spirit from our eyes. Shelley develops this symbol in his *A Defence of Poetry* and deepens the connotations of the metaphor even further when he remarks that "Poetry lifts the veil from the hidden beauty of the world, and makes familiar objects be as if they were not familiar." Similarly, it is not Mrs. Radcliffe's invention of a trick ending to the Gothic tale which insures her a place in the larger chronicles of literary culture and the history of Romanticism in particular. To be sure, the wild voices heard in the night are found to be the wind whipping through eroded battlements and the mysterious nocturnal melodies are always traced to a very real but concealed musician; yet this is not what caused De Quincey to call her a "great enchantress" or Keats to acknowledge her as "Mother Radcliffe." Rather, to paraphrase Poe, Radcliffe's terror is not of Italy but of the soul, and her horror is only a small part of the larger landscape of sensibility—of limitless spiritual and psychological "mystery"—which she was the first to enter and explore. Through her heroine Emily, Mrs. Radcliffe helped to spread suddenly open the gorgeous fan of the Romantic consciousness and accomplish what Wordsworth called "widening the sphere of human sensibility." Emily's voyage through the Alps and Appenines toward Udolpho becomes, then, another metaphor for that quest which the Romantics themselves cultivated and often internalized. This was a journey on which the Neo-Classic sensibility was unwilling to embark, as it kept strictly within the limits of a Reason which feared excesses of the imagination and an over-stimulation of the faculties of the soul. Indeed, Emily's unfortunate father, M. St. Aubert, a figure of melancholy common sense who warns Emily about the "evils of susceptibility" at the beginning of the *Mysteries,* actually has to alight from the coach when it pauses on its magic journey in order to renew his contact with the earth. Ostensibly, he crawls so intently over the landscape because, as a typical rationalist, he has a botanical passion for classifying (and so limiting the possibilities of) natural phenomena. Eventually, however, St. Aubert dies of the effects of the journey itself, a journey in which as it continues "the mountains seemed to multiply, as they went, and what was the summit of one eminence proved to be only the base of another," or, "the scene seemed perpetually changing, and its features to assume new forms, as the winding road brought them to the eye in different attitudes while the shifting vapours, now partially concealing their minuter beauties and now illuminating them with splendid tints, assisted in the illusions of the sight. It is of this constantly shifting confusion of the real and the ideal, of noumena and phenomena, of the dazzle of the veil, that M. St. Aubert finally expires, and, in truth, it can be said that he died, like the Age of Reason itself, of an overexposure to Romanticism. What Mrs. Radcliffe has done, with her pages and pages of landscape description which never seem to end (in which more and more sublime vistas continue to unveil themselves through the rolling mists and rainbow fogs), is to make the momentous connection between the life of nature and the life of the mind which made Romanticism itself into a true revolution of the human consciousness. Emily does not merely contemplate these sublime scenes, but she actually helps to create, through the ever-expansive faculties of her Romantic imagination, the mountains beyond mountains and the plains behind plains. Her mediumistic powers of reverie and feminine weaving of the warp of landscape with the woof of dreamscape are halted only by a traumatic confrontation with the dark and limiting male reality of Udolpho itself:

> Emily gazed with melancholy awe upon the castle, which she understood to be Montoni's; for, though it was now lighted up

by the setting sun, the gothic greatness of its features, and its mouldering walls of dark grey stone, rendered it a gloomy and sublime object. As she gazed, the light died away on its walls, leaving a melancholy purple tint, which spread deeper and deeper, as the thin vapour crept up the mountain, while the battlements above were still tipped with splendour. From these, too, the rays soon faded, and the whole edifice was invested with the solemn duskiness of evening. Silent, lonely and sublime, it seemed to stand the sovereign of the scene, and to frown defiance upon all, who dared to invade its solitary reign. As the twilight deepened, its features became more awful in obscurity, and Emily continued to gaze, till its clustering towers were alone seen, rising over the tops of the woods, beneath whose thick shade the carriages soon after began to ascend.

(Mysteries of Udolpho)

From a conveniently modern Jungian perspective, we could say that the Anima has here met the Shadow. Yet it was not for Mrs. Radcliffe to follow the profound implications of her method, for those implications were at once too dangerous and disturbing for her own retiring sensibility to sustain. Rather, it was for others, like Edgar Allan Poe (who, in his tale "The Oval Portrait," described the chateau to which the wounded narrator is brought as "one of those piles of commingled gloom and grandeur which have so long frowned among the Appenines, not less in fact than in the fancy of Mrs. Radcliffe) to explore fully those novel elements implicit in *Udolpho,* which were in fact the mysteries of the progress, experience, and destiny of the Romantic soul. In undertaking this quest, Poe also had to solve the problem which had eluded Mrs. Radcliffe in her own attempt to embody such a pilgrimage, for finally *The Mysteries of Udolpho* is subverted by its own freedom and eclecticism. The romance disintegrates from and succumbs to an imitative fallacy, an overindulgence in openness and limitlessness, as Emily becomes supplanted by another heroine the Lady Blanche, and Mrs. Radcliffe's own interests turn from the adventures offered by a picaresque travel narrative to the more genteel enchantments of a sentimental and well-bred fairy tale. This eclecticism and lack of definition, springing from the eternal process of Romantic reverie, was to plague as well such artists as Shelley, whose conflict of Demogorgan and Jupiter in *Prometheus Unbound* is a similar struggle of freedom with tyranny, as is the opposition between the Los and Urizen of Blake's late epics. The common Romantic problem remained the synthesis of an archetypal monomyth which would not destroy the surface mix and float of those novel elements which preserved the beauty and majesty of the free Romantic temperament. In specifically Gothic works of a less epic character, the further dilemma was to preserve the novelty, variety, and dark sensationalism which composed the fabric of the genre while also suggesting a profound spiritual and emotional depth. This is the enigma which challenged Poe when, in describing the effect of the sight of the House of Usher upon the narrator of his most famous tale, he wrote that, "It was a mystery all insoluble; nor could I grapple with the shadowy fancies that crowded upon me as I pondered."

Poe confronted this mystery in a typically "Gothic" way; that is, in spite of the fact that, as an anatomist of the imagination, he had mastered all of the genre's obvious popular elements and even felt some condescension toward it as a set of counters which he could manipulate at will, he decided to utilize in "The Fall of the House of Usher" its most radical manifestation for his own particular purposes. The most avant-garde of the Romantic revivals when he was writing the tale in 1839 was the Egyptian mode, and it is my contention that, in experimenting with a daring mixture of the Gothic and the Egyptian, Poe managed to create a work of art which fulfilled the search of the Romantics for a monomyth which functions at two distinct levels: the surface level of the picturesque, or the decorative, and the subterranean level of the subliminal and the archetypal. For, in resurrecting the Egyptian mode as part of the dramatic stage setting of his tale, Poe also revived the pattern of initiation ritual which underlaid the symbols of the Egyptian Mysteries, the Mysteries of Isis and Osiris, as they were understood by his own age. That ritual had already found its way into the ceremonies of the countless secret societies (such as the Masons and the Odd Fellows) which abounded in the America of the early nineteenth century. In *The Modern Eleusinia; or, The Principles of Odd Fellowship Explained by a Brother of the Order* (published in Nashua, New Hampshire, in 1844) the anonymous author, speaking of the Eleusinian Mysteries, expresses both a Romantic eclecticism and the fascination of his age at all levels with these "secrets of the soul":

> Their object seemed to be to teach the doctrine of one God, the resurrection of the good to eternal life, the dignity of the human soul, and to lead the people to see the Shadow of the Deity, in the beauty, magnificence, and splendour of the universe. The Mysteries of Isis . . . varied in some of their forms, from the Eleusinian, yet they all had one common design; namely, by the most solemn and impressive ceremonies, to lead the minds of the Neophytes, to meditate, seriously, the great problems of

human duty and destiny, to imbue them with a living sense of the vanity and brevity of life, and of the certainty of a future state of retribution, to set forth, in marked contrast, the beauty of Virtue and Truth, and the deep bitterness, and tormenting darkness of Vice and Error;—and, lastly, to enjoin on them, by the most binding obligations, charity, brotherly love, and inflexible honor, as the greatest of all duties, the most beneficial to the world, and the most pleasing to the Gods. By their rites, many of which we should now think rude and childish, rites commencing in gloom and sorrow, and ending in light and glory,—they dimly shadowed forth, the transition of man from the savage to the civilized state, from ignorance to science, and his constant progress, onward and upward through the Ages, to still sublimer revelations. By them, they also signified, that the soul's exaltation, and highest good, were to be approached, only by the way of tears, and sacrifice, and toil.

Here we have, optimistically and floridly, the outline of the same monomyth which is being enacted in the cavernous glooms of "The House of Usher." As Kathleen Raine notes in her *Blake and Tradition*, "The Eleusinian Mysteries were in fashion in and about 1790," and they soon merged with a general interest in things Eastern, Oriental, and especially Egyptian.

Little of the physical evidence of this Egyptian Revival remains with us today, though there were famous architectural examples such as "The Tombs" (a New York prison in Egyptian style in which Melville's Bartleby found his undeserved end) and we still have the towering obelisk of the Washington Monument as a witness to its brief but powerful influence on public taste. A popular interest in Egyptology had been spurred with the finding of the Rosetta Stone in 1799 by Napoleon's armies, and, after its cession to the British in 1801, it became, along with other Egyptian antiquities, almost as curious and sensational an exhibit as the Elgin Marbles were to be in 1807. The deciphering of hieroglyphics became the rage among antiquarians, and researches were carried on by a host of eminent scholars. Besides prison buildings, cemetery gates and entrances were done in a pylonic form copied from Nile temples, for, while the Gothic style of architecture was naturally associated with religious ideas of spiritual aspiration (hence its use for ecclesiastical and college buildings), the Egyptian mode was considered to be more suited for the contemplation of darker, more impenetrable mysteries. As Frances Lichten writes of this revival:

The first decorative inspirations derived from the contemplation of these archeological wonders seem weighted with immense solemnity—the Victorian architect, if not the Victorian designer, was sensitive to the portentousness of Egyptian art and used it for equally serious purposes, calculated to move the beholder to thoughts of death. Nor did he miss the correspondence of catacombs with the idea of prisons; therefore prisons styled in the Egyptian manner breathed forth their gloomy implications, even in the United States.

In American literature, as in American art and architecture, the Egyptian Revival produced no really lasting monuments and so always remained something of an underground style. But the Egyptian mode carried with it, as we have seen, a whole host of complex and intricate mythic associations, and it is my contention, to repeat, that many of these associations inform and help to shape the overall design of the Gothic castle or manor house of literature, which, like much of the architecture of its time, mixes Gothic arches with Egyptian obelisks. The haunted castles and mansions of such tales as Poe's "The Fall of the House of Usher" are, I believe, eclectic structures in which a Gothic frame is supported by a basically Egyptian foundation, and the mystery all insoluble of their effect has a direct relation to the larger Mysteries of Initiation into temple secrets concerned with the exaltation of the soul and its torturous rebirth.

I

The exact nature of these Egyptian Mysteries, meant to be imparted in the labyrinths of temple and pyramid, springs from the ancient religion which was practiced in Dynastic Egypt from an almost immemorial time until it was adopted, first by the Greeks, and then by the Romans. Finally, it reached an apex in the cult of Isis, which flourished in the world capitals of the early Christian era. Alexandria (the site of the Great Library whose volumes of sacred lore were later used by Arab invaders to fire the waters of the public bath) became the center for this mystery cult and the perpetuation of its ritual, as the sun god, Osiris, sacred to the pharaohs, was transformed into the more cosmopolitan and eclectic deity, Serapis. As Harold Willoughby summarizes in his study of Mystery initiations in the Greco-Roman world, *Pagan Regeneration,*

> The ancient system had centered in the god, Osiris; but in the reformed cult of Hellenistic times he was replaced to a considerable extent by a new divinity, Serapis, and popular interest was transferred to the more appealing personality of Isis. She dominated the Hellenistic cult quite as Demeter held the supreme

place in the Eleusinian mysteries, or the *Magna Mater* in those that emanated from Phrygia. In the ancient Osirian religion, the public ritual with its strong appeal to the masses was important. In the Hellenized worship of Isis, the significant ceremonials were those secret rites that had such deep meaning for the individual. These were only some of the ways in which the new cult showed adaptation to the very personal needs of individual religionists in the Hellenized world.

So in the first and second centuries A.D. the Mysteries of Egypt became the Mysteries of Isis, just as in the Dark Ages they were to become the Mysteries of Hermes, centering on alchemy and the transmutation of lead into gold as a means of symbolizing the tenets of basically the same esoteric ritual and philosophy. The Mysteries always involved a hieratic initiation into an arcane knowledge of immortality, knowledge achieved by a purification of the soul and a rite of passage through various prescribed trials and tests. It is a tribute to the truly sacred and secret character of this ritual that we know of its details only in fragments salvaged from ancient classical historians and a few Doctors of the Church. Even Herodotus, speaking of the performance of the Egyptian Mysteries at Saïs, felt constrained to tell his readers that "I could speak more exactly of these matters, for I know the truth, but I will hold my peace." What we do know, then, comes mainly from a handful of authors who are themselves the fathers of the occult tradition known generally as Hermeticism, which includes later alchemical and mystical commentaries as well as the few original texts which survived the wreck of the ancient world and the apparent extinction of learning during the early Middle Ages.

Poe's works, for example, contain learned references not only to Herodotus, Diodorus, and Plutarch, but also to Lucius Apuleius, who included in his *Metamorphoses* (better known in English as *The Golden Ass*) the most famous description of Isiac ritual which we possess. Apuleius, a Neoplatonic philosopher of the second century A.D., followed Plutarch's model in holding back the most sacred details of the initiation rite as "things too holy for utterance," for "both tongue and ear would be infected with like guilt did I gratify such rash curiosity." Poe also mentions such authors as Tertullian and Iamblichus, both of whom discussed the Mysteries in one form or another, and he makes further reference to Demeter and Isis, who were considered by Diodorus to be interchangeable forms of the same goddess (the reform of the Osiris cult merged many aspects of the native Greek Eleusinian Mysteries with the Mysteries of Egypt). In "A Descent into the

Maelström" there is even a reference by Poe to the seventeenth-century Jesuit occultist Athanasius Kircher. Kircher's most famous work was the massive *Oedipus Aegyptiacus* (1652), a compendium of Egyptian, alchemical, and kabbalistic lore which contained in its final volume a description of the Mensa Isiaca, a hieroglyphic stone tablet once thought to describe in detail the full process of initiation, which Kircher relates to the *De Mysteriis Aegyptiorum* of Iamblichus, among others. There were, too, already in existence literary transmutations of these sources, such as Jean Terrasson's eighteenth-century romance, *Sethos,* and Novalis's *The Novices of Saïs* (1798). Coming closer to the time of Poe, we could say, as H. Bruce Franklin says of Melville's knowledge of Egyptian myth, "For contemporaneous versions and explanations [he] could have opened the pages of innumerable magazines, travel books, encyclopedias, and polemical tracts."

But, for Poe, there is firm evidence of a more specific contemporary source for his acquaitance with a highly romanticized narrative of initiation into the Mysteries of Isis. In 1840, a year after "Usher" was published, Poe reviewed *Alciphron: A Poem* (1839) by the Irish poet Thomas Moore, who had already caught the public fancy for things exotic with his long Oriental fantasy *Lalla Rookh. Alciphron,* however, was only a redoing in verse of what Moore had already done in his short prose romance *The Epicurean* (first published in 1827), with which Poe was undoubtedly familiar, for in his review of *Alciphron* he mentions that the narrator is head of the Epicurean sect at Athens, a fact that is mentioned only in the romance and not in the poem. Burton R. Pollin has already traced the influence of *Alciphron* and *The Epicurean* on Poe's prose fantasy, "Shadow—A Parable," but no one has yet considered its influence on "The Fall of the House of Usher." For Moore's work provided not only that Romantic-Gothic eclecticism which gives the tale a novel and even sensational character, but also the underlying monomyth of initiation ritual which secretly unifies and deepens its metaphysical dimension.

Poe begins his review by praising Moore in no uncertain terms for his imaginative re-creation of a lost and exotic world, writing that "Amid the vague mythology of Egypt, the voluptuous scenery of the Nile, and the gigantic mysteries of her pyramids, Anacreon Moore has found all of that striking *materiel* which he so much delights in working up, and which he has embodied in the poem before us." Like Byron, Poe refers to Moore as "Anacreon," for in 1804 Moore had first made his name with a translation of the *Odes of Anacreon,* by the Classic poet famous for his short lyrics on the subjects of love and wine. Both *The Epicurean* and *Alciphron,* which Moore admits were directly influenced by Terrasson's *Sethos,* attempted to accomplish something much more ambitious, however. Poe's summary of the poem (which can stand for the romance as well) gives some indication of the scope of Moore's philosophical and antiquarian interest:

> The design of the story (for plot it has none) has been less a consideration than its facilities, and is made subservient to its execution. The subject is comprised in five epistles. In the first, Alciphron, head of the Epicurean sect at Athens, writes, from Alexandria, to his friend Cleon, in the former city. He tells him (assigning a reason for quitting Athens and her pleasures) that, having fallen asleep one night after protracted festivity, he beholds, in a dream, a spectre, who tells him that, beside the sacred Nile, he, the Epicurean, shall find that Eternal Life for which he had so long been sighing. In the second, from the same to the same, the traveller speaks, at large and in rapturous terms, of the scenery of Egypt; of the beauty of her maidens; of an approaching Festival of the Moon; and of a wild hope that amid the subterranean chambers of some huge pyramid lies the secret which he covets, the secret of Life Eternal. In the third letter, he relates a love adventure at the Festival. Fascinated by the charms of one of the nymphs of a procession, he is first in despair at losing sight of her, then overjoyed in seeing her in Necropolis, and finally traces her steps until they are lost near one of the smaller pyramids. In epistle the fourth (still from the same to the same) he enters and explores the pyramid, and, passing through a complete series of Eleusinian mysteries, is at length successfully initiated into the secrets of Memphian priestcraft; we learning this latter point from letter the fifth, which concludes the poem, and is addressed by Orcus, high priest of Memphis, to Decius, a praetorian prefect.

For our purposes, the most interesting segment of *The Epicurean* is chapters six to eleven, which, as Poe indicates, contain a full and highly dramatic rendering of an initiation into the Egyptian Mysteries. It is interesting, too, that Poe refers to these Mysteries as "Eleusinian," thus reflecting like the anonymous author of *The Modern Eleusinia*, the eclecticism which merged all these forms of secret cult worship under the general heading of "Egyptian secrets." The Eleusinian Mysteries centered on the myth of Persephone, daughter of the earth goddess Demeter, and her rape and abduction to the Underworld by the dark daemon god Pluto. Eleusinian ritual involved the symbolic interment of Persephone and a search for her by Demeter in a passion drama which was so similar to the death of the sun god Osiris and his enchainment by the evil force, Typhon, that Lucius Apuleius (in discussing the Mysteries of Isis) says of his initiation that "I drew near the confines of death, I trod the threshold of Proserpine, I was borne through all the elements and returned to earth again."

This examination returns us to the beginning of "The Fall of the House of Usher" and the effect of that structure and its surrounding landscape on the spirits of the narrator. For the sight of the House of Usher does not inspire awe and feelings of the sublime, but rather a shrinking dread and those dim apprehensions about impenetrable secrets, solemn catacombs, and morbid depths which Egyptian architecture was supposed to awaken in the Romantic mind. Indeed, the narrator confesses to experiencing only "an iciness, a sinking of the heart—an unredeemed dreariness of thought which no goading of the imagination could torture into aught of the sublime." The Gothic mode of architecture was an objective correlative, one might almost say, for a sublime response on the part of the onlooker. But in the Gothic mode of literature, the literature of horror, as it is sometimes called, the transcendent feeling of the sublime is replaced by a numinous, nameless dread. Poe's narrator cannot even torture his imagination into producing a minimally sublime transport, for in gazing upon the House of Usher, he has the same forebodings as those nineteenth-century Romantics who meditated upon the ruins of the Temple of Karnak or the Great Pyramid at Giza.

II

Let us turn, then, to a detailed consideration of this most famous of Gothic short stories. The opening of Poe's tale, I suggest, is in the general Romantic tradition of a meditation on ruins, made popular by such eighteenth-century works as Volney's *The Ruins; or, A Survey of the Revolutions of Empires* (1791), and popularized by countless nineteenth-century poets and graphic artists. In Poe's contemporary America, we need only to look to a series of paintings like Thomas Cole's *The Past* and *The Present* (1838), Asher B. Durand's *The Morning of Life* and *The Evening of Life* (1940), or John Vanderlyn's *Marius Brooding on the Ruins of Carthage* (1807) to find an appropriate aesthetic parallel. But Poe's meditation, I would again emphasize, is on a very particular kind of ruin, a ruin in which the Mysteries of Egypt and Isis have been, or are about to be, performed. This is the famous Gothic Waste Land which confronts the narrator of "Usher":

During the whole of a dull, dark, and soundless day in the autumn of the year, when the clouds hung oppressively low in the heavens, I had been passing alone, on horseback, through a singularly dreary tract of country, and at length found myself, as the shades of the evening drew on, within view of the melancholy House of Usher. I know not how it was—but, with the first glimpse of the building, a sense of insufferable gloom pervaded my spirit. I say insufferable; for the feeling was unrelieved by any of that half-pleasurable, because poetic, sentiment, with which the mind usually receives even the sternest natural images of the desolate or terrible.

The narrator continues his attempt to define the effect of these stern images on his spiritual faculties by concluding with an elusive but significant reference:

I looked upon the scene before me—upon the mere house, and the simple landscape features of the domain—upon the bleak walls—upon the vacant eye-like windows—upon a few rank sedges—and upon a few white trunks of decayed trees—with an utter depression of soul which I can compare to no earthly sensation more properly than to the after-dream of the reveller upon opium—the bitter lapse into every-day life—the hideous dropping off of the veil.

Like a skull half-sunk in the desert sands, or a sphinx partially uncovered by desert winds, the House of Usher confronts the narrator with the shock of a sepulchral *memento mori,* and, in describing its effect, he thinks automatically of a fragment of the Mysteries associated with Egypt, the land of death, sphinxes, and pyramids, and their reigning goddess, Isis. His phrase, "the hideous dropping off of the veil," refers to a motif better known to the early nineteenth century than to us, though it was revived, appropriately enough, in the 1870s by that grand mistress of the occult and esoteric, Madame H. P. Blavatsky, founder of the Theosophical Society. In her *Isis Unveiled, A Master-key to the Mysteries of Ancient and Modern Science and Theology,* which attempted to merge Eastern mysticism with the Western occult tradition founded on Hermeticism and Neoplatonism, Madame Blavatsky announced,

In our studies, mysteries were shown to be no mysteries. Names and places that to the Western mind have only a significance derived from Eastern fable, were shown to be realities. Rever-

ently we stepped in spirit within the temple of Isis; to lift aside
the veil of "the one that is and was and shall be" at Saïs, to look
through the rent curtain of the Sanctum Sanctorum at Jerusalem;
and even to interrogate within the crypts which once existed
beneath the sacred edifice, the mysterious Bath-Kol.

Madame Blavatsky finished her typically obscure rhetorical flourish
with a mention of the "Bath-Kol," the mysterious oracle of God which
certain rabbis maintained had spoken spontaneously within the precincts of
the Tabernacle at Jerusalem, but her reference to the veil of Isis has the
same source as Poe's reference to "the hideous dropping off of the veil" in
his description of the melancholy effect of the House of Usher. For, in his
treatise on the Egyptian Mysteries *De Iside et Osiride,* Plutarch, the first-
century Roman historian, had written of the Egyptian priesthood that

their philosophy is involved in fable and allegory, exhibiting
only dark hints and obscure resemblances of the truth. This is
insinuated, for example, in the sphinx, a type of their enigmatical
theology, and in such inscriptions as that engraved on the base
of Minerva's statue at Saïs, whom they regard as identical with
Isis: "I am every thing that has been, that is, and that shall be;
nor has any mortal ever yet been able to discover what is under
my veil."

Only those fully initiated into the cult of Isis, which conferred upon
her initiates the like status of godhood or immortality, were permitted to
lift the veil of Isis. Hence the equation by Poe's narrator of a sickness unto
death and ultimate despair with an unwarranted and blasphemous "hideous
dropping off of the veil." The reference, as mentioned in connection with
Radcliffe, was a common one in Romantic literature. Novalis writes in his
The Novices of Saïs, for example, that "I, too, then will inscribe my figure,
and if according to the inscription, no mortal can lift the veil, we must seek
to become immortal; he who does not seek to lift it, is no true novice of
Saïs." Thomas Moore, in *The Epicurean,* has his hero Alciphron say of Isis
(after he has arrived in Egypt to study "the mysteries and the lore") that
"At Saïs I was present during her Festival of Lamps, and read, by the blaze
of innumberable lights, those sublime words on the temple of Neitha;—'I
am all that has been, that is, and that will be, and no man hath ever lifted
my veil.' " And, as in Hawthorne's *Blithedale Romance,* where Zenobia
suggests by her legend of "The Silvery Veil" that the Veiled Lady's mysterious drapery might even conceal "the face of a corpse" or "the head
of a skeleton," *The Epicurean* contains an episode in which Alciphron

raises the veil of a strangely silent figure at a feast and finds it to be a hideous mummy.

Like the silver skeleton present at the banquet of Trimalchio in Petronius's *Satyricon*, the mummy is a reminder to remember death in the presence of life; and its effect on Alciphron is once again much like the effect of the House of Usher on Poe's narrator, for the Epicurean confesses, "This silent and ghostly witness of mirth seemed to embody, as it were, the shadow in my own heart." It is a witness, too, in much the same way in which the pyramids, as watchtowers of time, generate shadowy fancies in the mind of Alciphron when he contemplates the ruins of the monuments of Memphis. Usher's House, we might note, is also as mummified as the corpse of any emblamed pharaoh of the Dynasties, for Poe writes of its "extraordinary dilapidation" that

> there appeared to be a wild inconsistency between its still perfect adaptation of parts, and the crumbling condition of the individual stones. In this there was much that reminded me of the specious totality of old woodwork which has rotted for long years in some neglected vault, with no disturbance from the breath of the external air.

The total effect of the House of Usher on Poe's narrator, then, is paralleled by the effect of the Pyramids of Memphis upon Moore's Epicurean:

> There was a solemnity in the sunshine resting upon those monuments—a stillness, as of reverence, in the air that breathed around them, which stole, like the music of past times, into my heart. I thought what myriads of the wise, the beautiful, and the brave, had sunk into the dust since earth first saw those wonders; and, in the sadness of my soul, I exclaimed,—"Must man, alone, then, perish? must minds and hearts be annihilated, while pyramids endure? O Death! even upon these everlasting tablets—the only approach to immortality that kings themselves could purchase—thou hast written of our doom, awfully and intelligibly, saying,—'There is for man no eternal mansion but the grave.' "
>
> (*The Epicurean*)

Alciphron perhaps voices those thoughts too deep for tears which oppress Poe's narrator, who, gazing at the mansion of the Ushers, also thinks unconsciously of the "long lapse of centuries" and "the consequent undeviating transmission from sire to son, of the patrimony with the name, which had, at length, so identified the two as to merge the original title of the estate in the quaint and equivocal appellation of the 'House of Usher.' " The narrator, unable to articulate the feeling of insufferable gloom which causes such "an iciness, a sinking, a sickening of [his] heart," here matches Alciphron, who exclaims, "My heart sunk at the thought; and for the moment, I yielded to that desolate feeling, which overspreads the soul that hath no light from the future." It is precisely to exorcise this feeling that Alciphron undertakes his mission to undergo the trials of mystery initiation, in the hopes of gaining an immortality which will forever banish his fears about the vanity of human wishes and the transience of human accomplishment. The meditation on ruins thus merges naturally and imperceptibly with the immemorial *ubi sunt* tradition, but, whereas Alciphron manages to shake off his feeling of ultimate desolation, the same emotion continues to pervade and to permeate the atmosphere of the House of Usher, as well as to afflict its master, the unhappy Roderick.

If the House of Usher can be considered, in its effect at least, to be a structure of Egyptian dread and magnitude, combining the uses to which such an image was put by the Romantic mind—temple, crypt, and prison—then Roderick Usher is indeed the master of this temple, as well as its entombed Pharaoh and its holy prisoner. He is the priest-king, chief celebrant, and hierophant of its Hall of Labyrinths, the Osiris who must descend into the depths of night in order to be reborn again in mystic marriage with his sister-wife, Isis. As Harold Willoughby writes,

> According to ancient cosmology, the sun each night visited the subterranean regions. In the rite of initiation, therefore, the votary as a new Osiris made both the infernal and the celestial journey like the sun. At midnight he saw the sun brightly shine in the realm of the dead, and likewise he mounted up into the heavens and saw the gods celestial as well as the gods infernal. In doing all this he was but playing the part of the dying and rising god Osiris in the salvation drama of the Isis cult.
>
> (*Pagan Regeneration*)

In visiting the House of Usher, the narrator is also visiting the House of the Dead, being guided (like the neophyte of the Isis rituals) through the subterranean regions, the vaults and crypts within the pyramid or underneath the Temple of Isis itself: "A valet, of stealthy step, thence conducted me, in silence, through many dark and intricate passages in my progress to the *studio* of his master." This master, the true conductor of the mysteries, is, again, Usher himself, for his very name echoes the meaning of the term "hierophant," which, as Carl Kerényi tells us in his study of the Eleusinian rites, means the priestly demonstrator of the holy mysteries.

The narrator of "The Fall of the House of Usher" is an unwilling initiate who has failed to comprehend the significance of the Mysteries he has witnessed and the passion-drama in which he has participated. Thus, he reports his experience in Gothic terms which frame the narrative according to the conventions of the *Schauerroman,* the tale which is more of Germany than of the soul. He can be considered as a partially unreliable reporter, like those early Church Fathers, who talk of the initiation rites as only so much nonsense and pagan mumbo jumbo, more mystification than mystery. This latter supposition accounts for Usher's characterization of the narrator as a madman precisely before the climax of the ritual Usher has been enacting, with his sister Madeline playing the part of the Isis-Persephone figure. The narrator is "mad" precisely because he does not recognize, or realize, the import of the chance for divine wisdom and revelation, with the concomitant gift of immortality, which has been offered to him by the gods themselves.

The first part of "The Fall of the House of Usher" can thus be read as an esoteric or even subterranean performance of an Egyptian Mystery rite, with Usher assuming the part of the hierophant and the narrator as an uncomprehending witness. The story follows, indeed, the five stages of Mystery initiation outlined by Lewis Spence in his study *The Mysteries of Egypt.* The first part can be seen as the necessary steps of contemplation, purgation, and a journey through the higher and lower regions, while the climax can be considered as embodying the culminating aspects of union and rebirth.

III

Long discipline and contemplation were a requisite part of the initiation process itself. As Edouard Schuré writes of the questing neophyte:

> Before rising to Isis Uranus, he had to know terrestrial Isis, had to learn the physical sciences. His time was divided between mediatations in his cell, the study of hieroglyphics in the halls and courts of the temple, as large as a city, and in lessons from his teachers. He learned the science of minerals and plants, the history of man and peoples, medicine, architecture, and sacred music. In this long apprenticeship he had not only to know, but to become.

In this respect, the narrator is the apprentice and Roderick is the master of the peculiar Pythagorean discipline taking place within the Halls of the Temple which is the House of Usher. While in Egypt studying the Mysteries, Pythagoras was said to have learned the fundamentals of geometry and the theory of the celestial orbs as well as all that pertained to computation and numbers. These he used to construct his abstract philosophy of numerical and harmonic progression. Thus Poe's narrator says of his intimacy with the recesses of Usher's spirit, "We painted and read together, or I listened, as if in a dream, to the wild improvisations of his speaking guitar." We do get a more direct hint, however, as to exactly what texts are studied in the discipline. "Our books," he remarks,

> —the books which, for years, had formed no small portion of the mental existence of the invalid—were, as might be supposed, in strict keeping with this character of phantasm. We pored together over such works as the Ververt et Chartreuse of Gresser; the Belphegor of Machiavelli; the Heaven and Hell of Swedenborg; the Subterranean Voyage of Nicholas Klimm by Holberg; the Chiromancy of Robert Flud, of Jean D'Iandaginé, and of De la Chambre; the Journey into the Blue Distance of Tieck; and the City of the Sun of Campanella.

As T. O. Mabbott and others have noted, "All of Usher's library . . . consists of real books, and, although Poe may have seen few of them, they all concern in one way or another the idea that spirit is present even in inanimate things and that the world, or macrocosm, has relations to the the microcosm, man." The books have usually been seen as only an extension of Roderick's belief in the sentience of all things. Yet it is not the books themselves and their content (for some, like Klimm's *Subterranean Voyage,* are merely satirical studies in the vein of Swift's *Gulliver's Travels*) but rather their titles which take on an occult significance. Most of them deal with a journey to the underworld, and we have seen that the journey of the sun god Osiris to the infernal regions was a central part of Egyptian ritual. "I drew near the confines of death," said Apuleius, "I trod the threshold of Proserpine, I was borne through all the elements and returned to earth again." And, he adds to this mystic revelation, "I saw the sun gleaming with bright spendour at dead of night, I approached the gods above, and the gods below, and worshipped them face to face" (*Mysteries of Egypt*).

Swedenborg's *Heaven and Hell,* for example, deals not only with an occult theory of correspondences but also with "the gods above" and "the gods below" as seen face to face by this Swedish mystic. Most of the other titles in Usher's library concern subterranean journeys and what one should expect to find in these infernal regions, thus paralleling the most famous *vade mecum* to the underworld, the sacred Egyptian *Book of the Dead*. For the Mysteries performed in life were considered only as a prelude to the same ritual to be enacted after death. The descent into an artificial darkness in the Temple of Isis was thought to be a symbolic re-creation and anticipation of the descent of the soul into Hades through the Door of Death. As Plutarch wrote, "When a man dies, he is like those who are being initiated into the mysteries. . . . Our whole life is but a succession of wanderings, of painful courses, of long journeys by tortuous ways without outlet" (*Pagan Regeneration*). And Thomas Taylor, the eighteenth-century translator of so many mystic and Neoplatonic texts, added in his *Dissertation on the Eleusinian and Bacchic Mysteries* that "as the rape of Proserpine was exhibited in the shews of the mysteries, as is clear from Apuleius, it indisputably follows, that this represented the descent of the soul, and its union with the dark tenement of body."

What Lewis Spence has to say about the antiquity of the sacred Egyptian texts, however, may explain why Poe includes among the library titles in the dark tenement of the House of Usher such an item as Campanella's *City of the Sun*. "The Book of the Dead," he writes, "was preceded by the Pyramid Texts, which recount the manner in which Egyptian royalty succeeded to union with the God [Osiris]. His soul bathed in the sacred lake, he underwent lustration with Nile water, and he then crossed the Lake of Lilies in the ferryboat. He ascended the staircase of the sun and reached the city of the sun, after magically opening its gates by a spell, being announced by heavenly heralds" (*Mysteries of Egypt*).

The titles in Usher's library, then, comprise an esoteric guide to the underworld of Usher, itself a journey into the blue distance of Mystery initiation. This journey ends with a transcendent vision—the City of the Sun, the golden state of Isis unveiled, in holy union with her brother-husband Osiris, who himself has been resurrected after death and dismemberment by the ecliptic powers of darkness. These latter powers the Egyptians personified by the god Set, whom Greeks designated as the wind monster Typhon. In the Eleusinian Mysteries, which Poe obviously thought were identical with the original Egyptian rites, the liturgy charted the course of Persephone through the precincts of Hades, to which she had been abducted by the god of the underworld Pluto. In the passion drama performed in the labyrinths of the House of Usher, this shadowy part is taken by the physician who has in his keeping Roderick's sister. Madeline is temporarily interred in one of the numerous vaults within the main walls of the building, for, like Persephone, she will be resurrected in the return to life and union which is the hierogamic marriage of Isis and her hierophant, Roderick, acting the part of the reborn sun god.

The proper guide for the descent into these infernal regions is thus *The Book of the Dead*. As Spence tells us, this book "is a magical book, inasmuch as the sorcery of everyday life is placed at the disposal of the dead in order that they may escape destruction in the journey toward the Otherworld by means of spells and magical invocations" (*Mysteries of Egypt*). The chapters of this most antique of volumes describe the monsters and enemies that the dead soul will encounter in its wanderings, revealing their secret names which, when uttered, allow the soul to control a host of destructive demons. Thus "Belphegor," in Poe's eclectic catalogue of demonology, is the name of the Ammonitic devil who lurked in the shadows of rocks and crevices, seducing the daughters of Israel until he was openly denounced by the angry prophet Hosea.

Another important section of *The Book of the Dead* is devoted to the judgment of Osiris, in which the soul is interrogated by forty-two judges to determine whether it is fit to take equal station with the sun god or be devoured by the howling monster who waits without. The last three books mentioned as part of Usher's library function precisely as this kind of symbolic scripture, familiarizing the soul with the demons to be met in the coming infernal journey; and following, as *The Book of the Dead* should follow, the Pyramid Texts. The list even culminates in a work that can be translated quite literally as the book of "The Watches of the Dead." Poe's narrator continues:

> One favourite volume was a small octavo edition of the *Directorium Inquisitorium,* by the Dominican Eymeric de Gironne; and there were passages in Pomponius Mela, about the old African Satyrs and AEgipans, over which Usher would sit dreaming for hours. His chief delight, however, was found in the perusal of an exceedingly rare and curious book in quarto Gothic—the manual of a forgotten church—the *Vigilae Mortuorum secundum Chorum Ecclesiae Maguntinae.*

We have thus come to the trials, inquisitions, and tortures that the questing soul, the aspirant of the Mysteries, must face if he is to obtain the right to confront Isis unveiled, for the *Directorium Inquisitorium* cherished by Roderick is actually a work by Nicholas Eymeric de Gerone, inquisitor-general for Castile in 1356, which gives an account of the tortures of the

Inquisition. It is for this that the instruction, purgation, and discipline have been instituted and the reason that the arcana, the *Hiera* (the sacred objects), have been revealed to the narrator, who is to accompany Usher on the infernal journey in the same way in which the neophyte is conducted, or ushered, by the hierophant.

One of the most important of these arcana, prophetic of the entombment of the sun god, is the series of strange paintings which Roderick executes as part of the discipline which occupies his waking hours before the descent into the Underworld. As the narrator writes of the uncanny effect of these paintings,

> From the paintings over which his elaborate fancy brooded, and which grew, touch by touch, into vagueness at which I shuddered the more thrillingly, because I shuddered knowing not why;—from these paintings (vivid as their images now are before me) I would in vain endeavor to educe more than a small portion which should lie within the compass of merely written words. By the utter simplicity, by the nakedness of his designs, he arrested and over-awed attention. If ever mortal painted an idea that mortal was Roderick Usher. For me at least—in the circumstances then surrounding me—there arose out of the pure abstractions which the hypochondriac contrived to throw upon his canvas, an intensity of intolerable awe, no shadow of which I felt ever yet in the contemplation of the certainly glowing yet too concrete reveries of Fuseli.

The narrator refers here to the Swiss artist of the weird and the grotesque, friend of Blake and a fellow-illustrator of visions and nightmares. But Usher's paintings are abstract in the same way that his musical studies are intense, formal, and intricate, for they form part of the larger pattern of exact instruction in the larger monomyth of the Mysteries. They are also like the "scenic representations," the "chambers of imagery," which Thomas Moore's Alciphron has to pass through in order gain admittance to the sanctuary of Isis. Edouard Schuré, in his imaginative re-creation of an initiation ceremony, based on the same Romantic sources with which Poe was familiar, writes of one segment of the ritual that

> A Magus called a *pastophor,* a guardian of sacred symbols, opened the grating for the novice and welcomed him with a kind smile. He congratulated him upon having successfully passed the first test. Then, leading him across the hall, he explained the sacred

paintings. Under each of these paintings was a letter and a number. The twenty-two symbols represented the twenty-two first
Mysteries and constituted the alphabet of secret science, that is,
the absolute principles, the universal keys which, employed by
the will, become the source of all wisdom and power.

(The Great Initiates)

Schuré relates these arcana to the Tarot deck and suggests that the
Tarot cards themselves represent symbolic fragments of initiation into the
Mysteries of Egypt and Isis. Although only one of Roderick Usher's awe-
inspiring paintings is described (and it seems to have no relation to Tarot
symbolism), Usher does act as a *pastophor* in exhibiting it to the narrator.
The work fits into the chain of occult symbolism that is developed through
the titles of the books in Usher's library. As the narrator relates,

One of the phantasmagoric conceptions of my friend, partaking
not so rigidly of the spirit of abstraction, may be shadowed
forth, although feebly, in words. A small picture presented the
interior of an immensely long and rectangular vault or tunnel,
with low walls, smooth, white, and without interruption or
device. Certain accessory points of the design served well to
convey the idea that this excavation lay at an exceeding depth
below the surface of the earth. No outlet was observed in any
portion of its vast extent, and no torch or other artificial source
of light was discernible; yet a flood of intense rays rolled
throughout, and bathed the whole in a ghastly and inappropriate
splendour.

Usher's painting might be entitled "The Burial of the Sun," for (as
Willoughby has already noted, referring to the statement of Apuleius that
"I saw the sun gleaming with bright splendour at the dead of night") the
novice made the same journey as the sun god Osiris. *The Book of the Dead*
tells us that this journey involved a descent into the nether regions of night
and darkness and then an ascent up the golden staircase of the sky to final
enthronement in Heliopolis, the holy City of the Sun. Thus at the end of
his initiation into the Mysteries of Isis, Apuleius writes, "I was adorned
like the sun and made in the fashion of an image." Willoughby comments
of Lucius's symbolic resurrection that "This was essentially a rite of dei-
fication, and Lucius with his Olympian stole, his lighted torch, and his
rayed crown was viewed as a personification of the sun-god" (*Pagan Regeneration*). The ancient Egyptians called part of the original ritual which

centered around the resurrection of pharaoh as a representative Osiris figure "the Rite of the Golden Chamber," and it is just such a golden chamber which Usher limns—the inner vault, the *sanctum sanctorum,* the burial chamber of a pyramid and the tomb of a god.

The ghastly and inappropriate splendor of Usher's vault is paralleled, too, by the unearthly phosphorescence of a cavern that Moore's Alciphron stumbles upon as part of his Mystery initiation in the depths of a pyramid at the necropolis north of Memphis. Moore writes,

> While occupied in these ineffectual struggles, I perceived, to the left of the archway, a dark, cavernous opening, which seemed to lead in a direction parallel to the lighted arcades. Notwithstanding, however, my impatience, the aspect of this passage, as I looked shudderingly into it, chilled my very blood. It was not so much darkness, as a sort of livid and ghastly twilight, from which a damp, like that of death-vaults, exhaled, and through which, if my eyes did not deceive me, pale, phantom-like shapes were, at that very moment, hovering.
>
> (*The Epicurean*)

Usher's painting, I think, does not so much look forward to the development of modern abstract art and nonobjective expressionism as it looks backward to Pythagorean geometry and the mysterious labyrinths of the pyramids. It is not Usher, however, but his sister Madeline who is interred in such a vault, for, being the exact twin of her brother ("sympathies of a scarcely intelligible nature had always existed between them"), she undergoes the passion of Persephone, prematurely buried in the sinks of Hades, while he underrgoes the passion of Osiris, slowly being torn apart and dismembered while she struggles for resurrection in the tomb. Her malady, as Poe specifically tells us, is cataleptic in nature; and the first trial of the Mystery initiation was a literal simulacrum of the death of the neophyte and his wandering, as a lost and questing soul, through the infernal regions. Schuré even speaks of "the seeming cataleptic death of the adept and his resurrection," but that resurrection is accomplished only by the trials and tortures foreshadowed in a book like the *Directorium Inquisitorium*—trials which are ultimately "elemental" in nature.

Lucius Apuleius had said of his initiation into the cult of Isis that "I was borne through all the elements." The elemental trials which are common both to *The Epicurean* and "The Fall of the House of Usher," then, are the ordeals of earth, fire, water, and air. In Usher's case, the trial by earth is obviously the entombment of his sister Madeline in the crypt, as well as his own entrapment in the labyrinthine dungeon of the house of his fathers. Similarly, the trials by air, fire, and water all culminate in the whirlwind which gathers in the vicinity of the mansion at the end of the tale, and in the vaporish activity of the tarn, which is supercharged with a weird phosphorescence. The tarn thus becomes the molten barrier which must be passed or endured if the initiation is to be successful. The narrator describes the scene in the following terms:

> The impetuous fury of the entering gust nearly lifted us from our feet. It was, indeed, a tempestuous yet sternly beautiful night, and one wildly singular in its terror and its beauty. A whirlwind had apparently collected its force in our vicinity; for there were frequent and violent alterations in the direction of the wind; and the exceeding density of the clouds (which hung so low as to press upon the turrets of the house) did not prevent our perceiving the life-like velocity with which they flew careening from all points against each other, without passing away into the distance. I say that even their exceeding density did not prevent our perceiving this—yet we had no glimpse of the moon or stars—nor was there any flashing forth of the lightning. But the under surfaces of the huge masses of agitated vapor, as well as all terrestrial objects immediately around us, were glowing in the unnatural light of a faintly luminous and distinctly gaseous exhalation which hung about and enshrouded the mansion.

In this context, it is interesting to note that Set or Typhon, the legendary force of darkness that temporarily overcame Osiris, was often conceived of as a storm or whirlwind. In fact, in Jacob Bryant's *A New System; or, An Analysis of Ancient Mythology* (first published in 1774) the author says of the Greek Typhon (from which the modern term "typhoon" is partially derived), "By this was signified a mighty whirlwind, and inundation: and it oftentimes denoted the ocean; and particularly the ocean in ferment." Certainly the tarn of Usher is a ferment, an unholy ferment which combines all the elements of earth, water, fire, and air, though the narrator attempts to explain away such unnatural appearances by reassuring Roderick with the Radcliffean explanation that they "are merely electrical phenomena not uncommon—or it may be that they have their ghastly origin in the rank miasma of the tarn." In *The Epicurean* Alciphron's trial by the elements of air and wind can be profitably compared with the sound and fury of Poe's tempest and its effect on the beholders of this midnight cyclone. The glare of an unnatural light during the hours which should be consecrated to darkness may also again remind us of Apuleius and his testimony that "I saw the sun gleaming with bright splendour at dead of night." Moore writes of the trials of air and fire:

> Just then, a momentary flash, as if of lightning, broke around me, and I perceived, hanging out of the clouds, and barely within my reach, a huge brazen ring. Instinctively I stretched forth my arm to seize it, and, at the same instant, both balustrade and steps gave way beneath me, and I was left swinging by my hands in the dark void. As if, too, this massy ring, which I grasped, was by some magic power linked with all the winds in heaven, no sooner had I seized it than, like the touching of a spring, it seemed to give loose to every variety of gusts and tempests, that ever strewed the sea-shore with wrecks or dead; and, as I swung about, the sport of this elemental strife, every new burst of its fury threatened to shiver me, like a storm-sail, to atoms!
>
> (*The Epicurean*)

Thus is Typhon, the Lord of Winds, unleashed with the same power that, with its "impetuous fury," almost lifts the narrator and Usher off their feet in Poe's tale. The "brazen ring" is missing from Poe's version of the trials, but there is a "shield of brass" and a whole pattern of hierarchical symbolism (which centers on the progression of the planetary metals) embodied in the fanciful history which Poe calls the "Mad Trist" of Sir Launcelot Canning. This is the work which the narrator reads to Roderick at precisely the same time that Madeline frees herself from the tomb. Yet, beneath the Gothic exterior of this pseudo-Grail romance once again lurks another Egyptian Mystery—the art and science of transmuting these metals, known popularly as alchemy, which also helps to structure the monomyth of "The Fall of the House of Usher." I have already explored this connection elsewhere, but what is important about the "Mad Trist" in the context of the original Egyptian Mysteries is the fact that it functions as a pageant or dumb show of the trials and torments that the questing aspirant has to endure. The ordeals of entering the City of the Sun, the "palace of gold, with a floor of silver," include the struggle with the monster of doubt and will, the Dragon "of pesty breath," Typhon, and the successful confrontation with the obstinate hermit, the Master of the Mysteries, who holds the key to the gates of full initiation. At the same time, Madeline is enduring the trial of earth, the ordeals of the labyrinth, and the premature burial which shadows forth the death of the old self and the rebirth of a new, untrammeled soul. This struggle issues in the final Mystery which the narrator is permitted to witness, the full *hieros gamos* of priest and priestess, Osiris and Isis, Roderick and Madeline, which fulfills the paradox that absolute purity of soul can only be attained by a physical ravishment. Since both Madeline and Roderick have attained the status of gods, however, their union is a sublime, awe-inspiring one which the narrator chooses to report under the guise of a typical Gothic catastrophe, echoing that "utter astonishment and dread" which he first evinced upon his entry into the catacombs of Usher:

> As if in the superhuman energy of his utterance there had been found the potency of a spell—the huge antique panels to which the speaker pointed threw slowly back, upon the instant, their ponderous and ebony jaws. It was the work of the rushing gust—but then without those doors there *did* stand the lofty and enshrouded figure of the lady Madeline of Usher. There was blood upon her white robes, and the evidence of some struggle upon every portion of her emaciated frame. For a moment she remained trembling and reeling to and fro upon the threshold, then, with a low moaning cry, fell heavily inward upon the person of her brother, and in her violent and now final death-agonies, bore him to the floor a corpse, and a victim to the terrors he had anticipated.

The veil of Isis has been lifted, then, with sublime consequences for Madeline and Roderick, whose earthly tenement is superseded by the radiant glories of Heliopolis. But this revelation has only "hideous" repercussions for the narrator, who has failed to comprehend the full significance of the Mysteries he has witnessed. The closing scene of "The Fall of the House of Usher" is described in the terms of an apocalypse, a catastrophe like the archetypal Gothic climax of Horace Walpole's *The Castle of Otranto,* where a clap of thunder shakes the castle to its foundations, the walls are thrown down with a mighty force, and the poor witnesses think the last day is at hand. "There came a fierce breath of the whirlwind," the narrator of "Usher" exclaims, "—the entire orb of the satellite burst at once upon my sight—my brain reeled as I saw the mighty walls rushing asunder—there was a long tumultuous shouting sound like the voice of a thousand waters—and the deep and dark tarn at my feet closed sullenly and silently over the fragments of the 'House of Usher.' " This is not a description of an apocalypse, however, but of a new genesis, and it constitutes a conjunction rather than a catastrophe. Earth, water, air, and fire are now transcendently united, as Sun and Moon are sublimely conjoined. The initiation is complete, and, as the anonymous author of *The Modern Eleusinia* puts it, after the "deep bitterness, and tormenting darkness of Vice and Error," and "by the way of tears, and sacrifice, and toil," we have reached and actually witnessed "the soul's-exaltation."

IV

Beneath the Gothic tracery of the walls of "Usher" one can glimpse the massive Egyptian pylons which structure and support the House itself. But at the same time, we have traveled far from the hothouse Romanticism of Thomas Moore's *The Epicurean*, which points to the later Romantic decadence of works like *Salammbô*, *The Temptation of St. Anthony,* and *Salomé.* Beginning in the nostalgia and yearning for the past which was perhaps the strongest of the early Romantic senses, the Egyptian style soon degenerated into the felicities of historial romance, as the search for a unifying monomyth was similarly transferred from the realm of literature to the realm of science. Moore's *The Epicurean* is what we would have to term, without any pejorative meaning intended, mere romance; it illustrates the early fascination with the exotic and the eclectic which was to return in an even more overwhelming degree toward the last days of the Romantic Age.

What was lost in this shift was the traumatic connection between landscape and consciousness, the widening of the sphere of sensibility which conjoined the sense of place with the sense of self and which made the Romantic imagination into a new medium and a new universe, a metaphysical temple full of enchanting clerestoreys as well as demonic tunnels and howling labyrinths. Mrs. Radcliffe, in associating the landscape of the Alps and the Appenines with the high consciousness and snowy sensibility of her heroine, Emily, had begun all unwittingly a process which was to culminate in the daring use of metaphor which made the landscape of the House of Usher into a simulacrum of the desert places of the human soul. The "hideous dropping off of the veil" witnessed by the narrator was at one and the same time a privilege and a curse; a privilege for those, like Usher, prepared to go beyond the "trembling of the veil" (as Yeats titled his own autobiography) and a curse for those, like the narrator himself, who delved into the Mysteries of the soul without putting aside their rationalism, failing to realize that the precinct which they had entered was, in fact, holy ground. Thus is the narrator of "Usher" afflicted by shadowy fancies and an unfathomable melancholia at the beginning of Poe's tale and thus is he cursed with an unmediated Faustian knowledge at its end.

The quest for a monomyth involving the trials and progress of the soul was to become, as we have mentioned, more and more of a secular rather than a literary endeavor, as the eclecticism in which Romanticism began at last exhausted and subverted the Romantic consciousness itself. Beginning with the attempt of Athanasius Kircher to produce a compendium of occult knowledge in his *Oedipus Aegyptiacus* (1652–55), the scholarly synthesis of ancient religious history and the Mysteries of myth continued in a work we have already quoted, the enormously influential *A New System; or, An Analysis of Ancient Mythology* (published by Jacob Bryant in three volumes from 1774 to 1776). Poe was undoubtedly familiar with this work, for he refers to Bryant's "very learned 'Mythology' " in "The Purloined Letter," and in *Eureka* he quotes with approval Bryant's declaration that "Although the Pagan fables are not believed, yet we forget ourselves continually and make inferences from them as from existing realities." Bryant proceeded to reduce all antique mythologies to one grand monomyth, which could be traced to the primal event of the Flood, so that "All the mysteries of the Gentile world seem to have been memorials of the Deluge." Bryant's syncretism was continued by disciples such as George Stanley Faber, whose *Dissertation on the Mysteries of the Cabiri* (1803) bore the typical fulsome and self-explanatory subtitle: *Being an Attempt to Deduce the Several Orgies of Isis, Ceres, Mithras, Bacchus, Rhea, Adonis, and Hecate, from an Union of the Rites Commemorative of the Deluge with the Adoration of the Host of Heaven.* The historical quest, then, subsumed particular concerns with the nature and destiny of the individual soul in a general interest in mythology. The goal became the elusive monomyth that tied all myths together as a fossilized "epic of humanity" which portrayed the evolution from sympathetic magic to sophisticated religion. Sir James George Frazer climaxed this search in 1890 with the publication of the first two volumes of *The Golden Bough,* which was the virtuoso attempt of a trained classicist to solve the seemingly insoluble Mysteries of the Grove of Nemi.

Frazer, however, only resurrected and codified the occult and esoteric lore which had already provided such a treasure trove of eclectic symbolism for Romantics such as Moore and Poe. Moreover, Frazer also pointed to the connection between consciousness and landscape, between the individual and the magical environment which he inhabits, by emphasizing the legend of the Fisher King, whose psychic health and well-being ensured the fertility of his kingdom. The wounding of the King, who is also chief priest and hierophant—what Edouard Shuré calls "The Great Initiate"—causes his kingdom to lapse into decay and decline, producing the Gothic Waste Land which, as Stephen Mooney has pointed out, is common both to Eliot's famous poem and to Poe's "The Fall of the House of Usher." In the notes to *The Waste Land,* Eliot listed among the sources for his poem the "Adonis, Attis, Osiris" chapter of Frazer's *The Golden Bough,* which dealt in massive detail with the folklore of the Mystery religions, and especially with the role of the sacred marriage, which we have already discussed in relation to Poe. He also cited Jessie Weston's book on the Grail legend, *From Ritual to Romance,* as a direct inspiration for "the title, . . . the plan, and a good deal of the incidental symbolism of the poem."

From Ritual to Romance is a scholarly classic which attempts to prove that the Grail romances are derived from the vegetation rites of those same Mystery religions and that the main features of the Grail story—the Waste Land, the Fisher King, the Hidden Castle with its solemn Feast, and the Mysterious Feeding Vessel, the Bleeding Lance and Cup—are elements transmuted from the original monomyth of initiation ceremonies. Under this rubric, Usher, with his obscure illness and impotence, is also of course another kind of Fisher King, while the House itself becomes the Hidden Castle or sinister Chapel Perilous and its surrounding landscape of decayed and noxious vegetation is the Perilous Cemetery or Waste Land noted by Mooney. The "Mad Trist" of Sir Launcelot Canning (the title of which is reminiscent of *The Geste of Syr Gawaine,* another Grail romance mentioned by Miss Weston) continues the chivalric imagery, for the trencher or ringing brass shield that Poe's hero Ethelred must win is very like the sacred vessel of the Attis rite, which, as she points out, was both tympanum and cymbal. Weston concludes that the Grail romances are veiled accounts of Mystery initiations and she deduces that

> The earliest version of the Grail story, represented by our Bler-heris form, relates the visit of a wandering knight to one of these hidden temples; his successful passing of the test into the lower grade of Life initiation, his failure to attain to the highest degree. It matters little whether it were the record of an actual, or of a possible, experience; the casting into romantic form of an event which the story-teller knew to have happened, had, perchance, actually witnessed; or the objective recital of what he knew *might* have occurred; the essential fact is that the *mise-en-scène* of the story, the nomenclature, the march of incident, the character of the tests, correspond to what we know from independent sources of the details of this Nature Ritual. The Grail Quest was actually possible then, it is actually possible to-day, for the indication of two of our romances as to the final location of the Grail is not imagination, but the record of actual fact.

Poe's narrator, too, passes, or at least beholds, the first trials of initiation like the wandering knight at the threshold of the hidden temple, but his failure to recognize the full significance of the esoteric symbolism and ritual displayed by the hierophant loses him his chance for the highest degree. Indeed, the whole ambiguous narrative technique of "The Fall of the House of Usher" is implicit in Weston's description of this earliest of the Grail romances. When we turn to Eliot's *Waste Land* (which is an attempt to write another variety of *Modern Eleusinia* by imposing an occult monomyth on the chaos of contemporary life), we find the same kind of allusions to the presence of profounder Mysteries. The Egyptian mode surfaces in the name and practice of Eliot's sleazy fortune-teller, Madame Sosostris, and in her wicked pack of cards, the Tarot deck; to Weston, as to Schuré, there was no doubt that "parallel designs and combinations" of Tarot symbolism "were to be found in the surviving decorations of Egyptian temples" (*From Ritual to Romance*). Adding to the Egyptian symbolism, Eliot also utilized Far Eastern and Oriental sources, constructing a modern eclecticism which actually dramatized the search for meaningful archetypes in much the same way that Weston and Frazer used comparative techniques in their anthropological studies, or, though Eliot would have been horrified at the suggestion, much as Madame Blavatsky had sought for the monomyth amid all the esoterica of her *Isis Unveiled*.

What remains important is the fact that, while the unifying legend of the Grail romance and its occult meaning, uncovered by Frazer and Weston, made the quest for a monomyth possible again for Eliot in 1922, it was also possible for Poe in 1839. Ultimately, Poe and Eliot have the same sources and the same concerns, for, like all modern seekers for that myth (whether literary or anthropological), they try to reverse the direction of the quest away from romance and back toward ritual, that task which Jacob Bryant defined in his subtitle of *A New System; or, An Analysis of Ancient Mythology* as the attempt "to divest Tradition of Fable; and to reduce the Truth to its Original Purity." An awareness of this tradition, in turn, may force us to realize that, given its antecedents, *The Waste Land* is more truly "Gothic" in character than its first readers ever imagined. But the tradition also demonstrates that Poe, in successfully using the monomyth of initiation ritual to structure and to deepen the vital eclecticism of "The Fall of the House of Usher," was not only an adept of Gothic prestidigitation, but that he had mastered as well the most complex thaumaturgies of Romantic art.

The Ironic Double in Poe's "The Cask of Amontillado"

Walter Stepp

In Poe's "The Cask of Amontillado," a heraldic emblem offers a suggestive entrance into the story. Descending into the catacombs of Montresor's failed family, Fortunato says, "I forget your arms." It is one of his numerous blind, unintentional insults. The proud Montresor, biding his time, blinks not and replies: "A huge human foot d'or, in a field of azure; the foot crushes a serpent rampant whose fangs are embedded in the heel."

> "And the motto?"
> "Nemo me impune lacessit."
> "Good!" he said.

The brief scene highlights the major plot dynamics of Poe's great story: the clumsy insult, Montresor's menacing irony, and Fortunato's further blindness to this irony. ("Good!") Montresor flashes countless "clues" like the one above before Fortunato's rheumy eyes—signals of his impending doom, but Fortunato does not perceive. The clues are part of the larger "system" or "demonstration" motif of the story: Montresor, the diabolical rationalist, systematically demonstrates again and again that the arriviste, Fortunato, does not *know,* cannot distinguish. Montresor, at the end of his life, has addressed his narrative to "You, who so well know the nature of my soul," and it is as if he were performing before some ultimate audience, saying, "You see? I show him the picture of his own death, and he says 'Good!' " An unspoken corollary of this speech I have imagined for him might read, "And yet, this buffoon, this Fortunato . . . 'is rich, respected,

From *Studies in Short Fiction* 13, no. 4 (Fall 1976). © 1977 by Newberry College.

admired; he is happy, as once I was.' *He* is the heir of Fortune!" And so Montresor proceeds to demonstrate the illegitimacy of this heir.

The heraldic emblem represents all the irony of life that Fortunato cannot comprehend. But it is the more interesting, I think, for what it says of Poe's knowledge of his evil protagonist (the two being so often equated in Poe's case). For the emblem suggests a deeper motivation that Montresor does not understand, either, but which Poe seems to have built upon. The Latin verb in the motto makes clear what is clear anyway—that Montresor identifies himself with the golden foot, ponderously triumphing over the lashing serpent. When he holds up the dire image before Fortunato's unseeing eyes, he has in mind no doubt the golden legitimacy of his vengeance, a just and unquestionable retribution for the thousand lacerations he has borne in silence. He will tread him into the ground, and indeed he does seal poor Fortunato in stone.

Such is Montresor's reading of the emblem, it seems reasonably clear; but another reading—Poe's, I think—does not so easily identify Montresor with the foot. The snake is the more obvious choice. Secrecy, cunning, serpentine subtlety—these are the themes Montresor demonstrates best of all. And the huge, golden boot fits very snugly the Fortunato that Montresor presents to us—large, powerful, and very clumsy. The larger story shows very well how to read the emblem: a giant has blindly stepped on a snake.

Moreover, to arrive at my main point, the emblem represents a scene of mutual destruction. Allegorically speaking, the foot and the serpent are locked together in a death embrace: neither can escape the ironic bond that is between them. Through this allegory, then, I want to point to the deeper relationship between the two men, a deeper motive for murder, and, finally, a deep, ineffably horrible sense of retribution for the crime. This last may be especially difficult to see, in view of the fact that much of the slow horror of the tale derives from just that sense that Montresor has indeed escaped retribution for his deed, that he has acted out his readers' most terrible fantasy: to murder "without conscience." This is the chief burden of his demonstration, told with appropriately dry matter-of-factness. He ends by letting us know he has lived fifty triumphant years since the murder of "the noble Fortunato." My allegory, then, is certainly not Montresor's.

Is it Poe's? I shall say that Fortunato rather ironically represents the familiar Poe *doppelgänger,* and that, as in Poe's earlier, more explicit allegory, "William Wilson," the double corresponds with conscience. (That "with" is a nice hedge for the moment.) The correspondence is unmistakably pat in the earlier story; "Cask" suggests that Poe's command of his theme has considerably deepened in that the double now is a reversed image—a "negative" double, if you will, an ironic double. (Well, all doubles are; I mean something further in that the double is not recognized "as such" by Montresor.) I think most readers have noticed the rather perfect symmetry of opposition between Montresor and Fortunato; most readers should, for that is the chief burden of Montresor's systematic demonstration. Montresor frames a "facade-system" to deny his double, the irony being that he denies him so systematically that he ends by creating a perfect double-in-reverse. The analogy with a photographic positive and its negative is rather exact here—not because life operates so, but because of Montresor's compulsive program, his obsessional wish to demonstrate that "He is not I." Or: "I am not he." The right emphasis ought to emerge from the demonstration to follow.

I think I need mention only a few instances of the systematic oppositions that Montresor's procrustean method presents to us, enough to recall its obsessive symmetry. Most importantly, Fortunato is broadly drawn as a character entirely befitting his carnival motley and clownish bells. He appears as the open, gullible extrovert, an innocent possessed of that same ignorant vanity that caused the original fall from grace; he thinks he knows enough to sample the apple the serpent tempts him with. He believes the sacred Amontillado is meant for *him*, but he is a drunkard, Montresor lets us know, certainly not a man of his companion's fine taste. Every delicacy, every pearl of ironic distinction, is utterly lost on this man: "He is not I; I am not he."

But it should be said that Montresor more than once obliquely acknowledges that there is more to Fortunato than his portrait is designed to show. Montresor does acknowledge certain sympathies with Fortunato, which point to what is being denied by the rationalist's demonstration. He begins, "He had a weak point—this Fortunato—although in other regards he was a man to be respected and even feared." Here at least, in the beginning, Montresor is quite conscious of his portraiture's limitation, and perhaps that is enough to convince us that he is not himself caught up in his own "sincerity"—Montresor's word for his rival's weakness: "In painting and gemmary, Fortunato, like his contrymen, was a quack, but in the matter of old wines he was sincere." Montresor plays on this sincerity even as Fortunato practices on gullible millionaires. Fortunato is hoist by his own petard, and Poe intimates that Montresor is too, I think; but of course the mine of irony lies deeper with him. If Fortunato's "sincerity" is his connoisseurship, Montresor's is his system. But that is the larger point; here let me emphasize their clearer level of affinity: they are both successful "quacks."

"The rumor of a relationship"—the phrase is from "William Wilson"—sifts out in a few of Montresor's oft-noted "slips." One most touching occurs when Fortunato is near death. Montresor speaks of "a sad voice, which I had difficulty in recognizing as that of the noble Fortunato." The epithet may be taken as an obvious piece of sarcasm in keeping with the general ironic tenor, but I do not find that Montresor allows himself the double-edge when addressing "you who so well know the nature of my soul." Then he keeps to hard, dry understatement of fact. (An exception might be Montresor's final utterance: "*In pace requiescat.*" And even then, if there is indeed a bond between them . . .)

And most readers have noted this piece of apparent rationalization: "There came forth [from out the niche] only a jingling of bells. My heart grew sick—on account of the catacombs." There is also Montresor's failure to satisfy the "definitive" conditions he has set down for himself, the code of honorable vengeance. "A wrong is unredressed when retribution overtakes its redresser," Montresor says, and whether he satisfies that clause is being debated here. "It is equally unredressed when the avenger fails to make himself felt as such to him who has done the wrong." Satisfaction is not debatable here; Montresor fails, for of course Fortunato never knows why he dies. He does not know the avenger "as such." Indeed, his nemesis has gone to great lengths to show that Fortunato is not *capable* of knowing such a man. He merely knows that Montresor has deceived him and that his fortune has run out. To connect with our larger theme, then, Montresor has failed "definitively" to achieve his vengeance in a way that suggests he does not understand its motive much more than does Fortunato. Why *did* he fail? It would have been simple enough to state the formal motive: You have wronged me thus and so; therefore you die. Whether we explain it as a prideful blindness (system always assumed its rationale is self-evident) or as an unwillingness to raise the ambiguous question, the irony of Montresor's "oversight" derives deep from the common substance of the two apparently opposed characters. As the emblem foretold, Montresor is bound with Fortunato and "dies" with him.

But it is the "mocking echo" motif that is most suggestive of the two men's relationship. (I take the phrase from Hawthorne's "Young Goodman Brown," another kind of double story.) Montresor's chosen method of demonstration and torment is to resound Fortunato's innocent words, striking a sinister edge in them known only to himself and his sole confidant, his reader. I am suggesting something further, a strange case of what one might call "murderous identification." I am thinking of the obvious case of "William Wilson," in which the protagonist learns too late the retribution for slaying one's conscience. Two examples: When Fortunato at last realizes his murderer's intentions, he vainly tries to humor him.

> "But is it not getting late? Will they not be awaiting us at the palazzo, the Lady Fortunato and the rest? Let us be gone."
> "Yes," I said, "Let us be gone."
> *"For the love of God, Montresor!"*
> "Yes," I said, "for the love of God!"

And Fortunato is heard no more, silenced at last by his own words thrust back at him. Certainly the most horrific—because so understated—example of this diabolical doubling occurs immediately preceding this last. While Montresor has been laying the tiers of his masonry, Fortunato has been sobering up and presumably comprehending the imminence of his death; "a low moaning cry from the depth of the recess. It was *not* the cry of a drunken man." This is followed by a long and "obstinate" silence. When the wall is nearly completed, "A succession of loud and shrill screams, bursting suddenly from the throat of the chained form, seemed to thrust me violently back." Montresor quickly puts down his momentary fright and reassures himself of the "solid fabric of the catacombs." Then, "I reapproached the wall, I replied to the yells of him who clamored. I re-echoed—I aided—I surpassed them in volume and in strength. I did this, and the clamorer grew still." I have always wanted to see a skilled actor play that scene; rather, two skilled actors. Fine points matter especially here, to see in Montresor's performance just the fine, ironic blend of "quackery" and "sincerity." Fortunato's dazed agony would be a study, too, as he witnesses the weird spectacle of this devil out-clamoring his victim's agonies—eerie harmonics there. And perhaps in this terrible way, Montresor demonstrates how one defeats the double—by beating him at his own game, doubling *him* up. Just as the subtler quack dupes the lesser, so perhaps Montresor "re-echoes" an "echoer."

Again, the parallel with "William Wilson" helps here. There it was the uncanny voice of the double-as-conscience that was most devastating. *"And his singular whisper, it grew the very echo of my own."* But William Wilson was not so well defended as Montresor; he tried the direct frontal assault and lost. Montresor, it would seem, achieves his triumph by reversing roles with his double, in effect *usurping* the double's occupation. Now *he* becomes the menacing echo and sends his double to the doom meant for himself, as it happened to Wilson.

By systematically denying every impulse represented by "the noble Fortunato," Montresor perhaps restores the perfect, lucid order that prevailed when the Montresors "were a great and numerous family." That is to say, a mental equilibrium, false though it may be, has been restored. I am speculating now that the decline of the Montresor family represented a devastation of disorder to the compulsive Montresor, signifying to him the price of his impulsivity. I suggest this term, of course, because it is the direct antithesis of the cool, controlled character Montresor represents himself to be. I have tried to show Montresor's ambivalence toward the impulsive parvenue, the childlike Fortunato, indeed innocent to the end since he never "knows." As in "William Wilson," Montresor is "galled . . . by the rumor of a relationship," but in spite of the double's "continual spirit of contradiction, I could not bring myself to hate him altogether." Who is "the noble Fortunato"?

In "William Wilson," Poe makes it absolutely clear that the double represents conscience; such a parallel is not clear in "Cask," but it is the case, I think. Fortunato is not the interdictory conscience of "William Wilson," but he is conscience-related: he is guileless, trusting innocence. It may be misleading to call him conscience, but *his* death is required to slay conscience. If it is not so clear that Fortunato corresponds to conscience, perhaps the blame (or credit) may be laid to Montresor's elaborate plan of denial. If Fortunato is a double-as-conscience, such an idea is not likely to be directly verified by a man whose one great wish is to portray himself as a man—nay, *the* man—without conscience. Indeed, the murder of Fortunato might be thought of as a "test case" to confirm just that notion: a man kills his conscience and rests in peace for fifty years. Surely the horror of Poe's little gem rests on the fantasy of the crime without consequences. If a man might do that, as every boy has dreamed of doing, where is "the public moral perspective"? The disposal of a rival becomes as simple as a child's "omnipotent" wish that he should "go away."

"William Wilson" tells the story of a man who murdered his conscience and thus himself; the same story is at work in "Cask," I submit, but with the great difference that Wilson recognizes his folly, while Montresor steadfastly refuses to. This significant difference is at least one reason why I find "Cask" much the more interesting story. Wilson's recognition satisfies, perhaps too easily, our own conscientious understanding of the way things ought to be; Montresor is more difficult, he challenges that understanding. He makes claims on us, if we take him seriously, that Wilson does not. Wilson, for all his prodigality, is, after all, "one of us," the difference being of degree. But Montresor, like Iago, stands in the line of Machiavellians who assert that the public moral perspective is but a façade by which knaves are stung and puppies drowned. We may say that Montresor is at heart a tormented sinner like Wilson, but it requires rather than subtlety to show it, and the villain is not likely to own it when we do.

The question of "comeuppance" in the two stories is a measure of their relative subtlety. In "William Wilson," poetic justice is clear if not profound: He slew his conscience and thus himself. Poe clearly emphasizes an allegorical understanding, and his story serves that purpose admirably well. In "The Cask of Amontillado," the same idea is intimated, but much more ambiguously and with formidable qualifications that make its meaning less easily satisfying. That is, though a reader may discern significant chinks in Montresor's armor, the armor remains—for a lifetime, he tells us. The armor represents a powerful lie, and it is important not to underestimate its power. Its felt presence stands in defiance of any mere allegorical, or purely intellectual, understanding. It is disturbing, it sustains the muted horror of this story, and is not as easily dismissed, I think, as in James Gargano's formulation: "With a specious intellectuality, common to Poe's violent men, Montresor seeks to escape from his own limitations by imagining them as imposed upon him from beyond the personality by outside force. But the force is a surrogate of the self, cozening [the] man toward damnation with all the brilliant intrigue Montresor uses in destroying Fortunato." All which I most potently believe, but I hold it not honesty to have it thus set down, as Hamlet replies to *his* own speech. In the "damnation" of the criminal Montresor, I believe, in theory. Theological grounds being what they are not these days, I might make the case in the good humanistic tradition Gargano espouses. To gain precision and authority, I might go further to document, on psychoanalytic grounds, the suffering that must lie at the heart of "the compulsion neurotic." (I think that is the correct classification.) But, alas, these are general and even problematic premises; they do inform my understanding of Poe's story, but they tend to pale before the immediacy of Montresor's defiant evil. The truth of the story, its meaning, must acknowledge that dilemma of the reader—unless, of course, as is common, we want merely to use the story as "case" to illustrate doctrine. The slow horror of the story rests ultimately on the reader's ambivalent wish-belief that Montresor did indeed triumph, that he did indeed sin with impunity: that he *did* slay his conscience. When Poe had Montresor address his story to "you, who so well know the nature of soul,"—alluding perhaps to the *reader's* role as ironic double—I do not think he intended an easy irony.

Poe and Tradition

Brian M. Barbour

When Poe began as a creative artist in the late 1820s, there was no living American literary tradition for him to inherit. This is why scholars as diverse as Campbell and Davidson, seeking to reverse Baudelaire's ahistorical impetus, have turned inevitably to Coleridge in an effort to link Poe to the ideas of his time. There is nothing factitious about this as there was, perhaps, about Marshall McLuhan's effort thirty years ago to relate Poe to a Ciceronian ideal in the South: Coleridge had the most seminal mind of his century and Poe, particularly (but not exclusively) in his criticism, consciously adapted himself to the greater figure. But writers inherit more than just other writers, and Malraux's well-known dictum to the effect that it is the beautiful painting not the beautiful smile that inspires the artist is no more than a half-truth, good for the beginner without question but inapposite to the mature artist whose work grows out of, even as it seeks to correct, the life around him. L. C. Knights put it this way: "Now the possibilities of living at any moment are not merely an individual matter; they depend on physical circumstances and (what is less of a commonplace) on current habits of thought and feeling, on all that is implied by 'tradition'—or the lack of it." As applied to Poe, this sense of tradition—current habits of thought and feeling and their related values and ideals—is both wider and more exclusive than the conventional sense: wider because literature is only part of social experience, more exclusive because its focus will be primarily American.

From *The Southern Literary Journal* 10, no. 2 (Spring 1978). © 1978 by the Department of English of the University of North Carolina at Chapel Hill.

Poe's creative years coincided with the Age of Jackson, and it was within and against that tradition that his own sensibility developed. As a gifted artist he was alive to its weaknesses and limitations and saw more clearly than most where it fostered and where it thwarted human possibility, including normal sympathetic existence. Values and ideals lie at the center of tradition. "The central value of American culture in the early nineteenth century," John William Ward has argued, was "the assertion of the worth of the totally liberated, atomistic, autonomous individual." The strongest tradition shaping society, in other words, denied both the efficacy of tradition and the reality of society. If this was sometimes a paradox, the times had given it proof. The resulting tendency was to locate the experience of being in the exercise of the will; making straight the way was a certain utilitarian sense of mind, a kind of didactic rationalism that emphasized the immediate solving of practical problems and derided speculation. The drive was towards domination by the self rather than towards integration with other selves and the consequent modifications of ego-assertion. Means usurped ends and rather easily, for the moral consequences of the will-to-dominate of the autonomous self were kept conveniently obscure by the utilitarian theory of mind. It is against these features of the prevailing tradition that Poe needs to be seen. Lewis P. Simpson has shown that the search for an ideal literary *order,* growing out of his ever-projected magazine and exfoliating as an effective influence on American civilization, is the substratum underlying and unifying Poe's whole career. This vision, like his personal psychological experience, set him against any uncritical acceptance of the emerging ethos.

His most valuable stories *embody* a critique of this tradition. "The Purloined Letter," as we shall see, has a dialectical structure in which an outlook is criticized by means of a positive value actually present, but this is not Poe's customary method. His task was to show his society that its central values were not humanly adequate (or, at least, that they contained unsuspected dangerous consequences) and that its ordinary way of thinking kept this out of view. The consensus ran all the other way. In the practical and material realm what Ward calls the central value was well established, having received its classic expression in Franklin's *Autobiography.* Now in the spiritual and intellectual realm Emerson was striving to redefine the *opportunity* offered by the American experience, but with the same emphasis on the atomistic, autonomous self. As Professor Ward has noted, "No less than Jackson, . . . Emerson held a vision of the good society which had at its center the atomic individual, moving freely and without constraint through space and society, dependent upon nothing beyond his own personality and unaided self." The strongest moral voice within the culture was divided in its effect. Emerson was attacking American materialism, but he possessed no coherent social theory; by exalting atomism and individual will he unwittingly strengthened the development of society along lines in which materialism and will-to-dominate were increasingly normative and morally reputable. There was, in short, no effectively established critical position even identifying the fundamental problems. None, that is, outside the great fiction of the period, for the creators of Hurry Harry, Aylmer, Ahab, and Montresor were not deceived about the nature of the self-willing, means-obsessed, atomistic individual. But this fiction had not yet established itself as part of a tradition, for Americans were not yet sophisticated enough to see that profound moral insight was available in "stories."

What habits of thought and feeling would the emerging tradition engender? What were its consequences, beyond the immediate, for human life? Poe's basic technique arose as a way of exploring this tradition without having a recognized countertradition to invoke. It has to be said that the strangeness of his tales often mitigated their intended moral effect, although this was intended to provide a certain stark clarity. His most characteristic tales embody the central value of the self-willing, atomistic, autonomous individual, but they wrench us out of the lenitive atmosphere of American optimism to focus our attention on narrators whose willfulness expresses deep disorder within. We are obliged to see the moral consequences, the dark, hidden possibilities in what we believe. They force us to live through a world empty of nourishing relationships where characters exist in an atomistic void, condemned to the resources of their autonomous selves, a world in which no one is recognized as a person. Two steady, interdependent criticisms are brought to bear: the tradition frustrates the person's growth to wholeness, even leaving, in the emphasis on domination as opposed to integration, a basic and dangerous confusion over what it means to be human; and the utilitarian habits of mind keep this growth obscured, unfelt, and unprepared for. . . .

We are faced with an embarrassment of riches. To fully analyze Poe's finest stories along the lines I have been indicating would extend this paper to Gibbonian lengths. For convenience, therefore, I would like to concentrate on four tales, examining them in some detail; two—"The Purloined Letter" and "The Fall of the House of Usher"—convey Poe's analysis of the American mind, and two—"The Cask of Amontillado" and "Ligeia"—

display his insight into the will-to-dominate of the autonomous individual and its destructive consequences. Before proceeding, however, a word about the narrators. "The Purloined Letter" is unusual not only for its dialectic but also because the narrator is not the real subject. The most liberating moment in the history of Poe studies came when James Gargano demonstrated conclusively that Poe "often so designs his tales so as to show his narrators' limited comprehension of their own problems and states of mind; the structure of many of Poe's stories clearly reveals an ironical and comprehensive intelligence critically and artistically ordering events so as to establish a vision of life and character which the narrator's very inadequacies help to 'prove.' " The popular view of Poe as the exotic creator of *frisson* identified him with his narrators, but in fact the tales are, so to speak, told against them. This accounts for the wide diversity of styles, for he invented ways to convincingly communicate the feel of a variety of psychic disorders. And the function of the ironic structure is to open a moral perspective upon the experience.

"The Purloined Letter" is the last of those three tales—"The Murders in the Rue Morgue" and "The Mystery of Marie Roget" are the others—in which Poe is commonly recognized to have invented detective fiction. Holmes liked to point it out to Dr. Watson as a salutary lesson, and the argument that they two descend from Dupin and Poe's narrator—that the basic elements and configuration of the genre sprang Minerva-like from his head—is a familiar one. These tales are ordinarily called "ratiocinative," but the term is misleading inasmuch as it suggests that what is of greatest importance is a method of Holmes-like deduction whereby Dupin outwits the Minister D——. That piece of detection largely serves as a framework within which Poe can explore the question, What constitutes real intelligence?

Like many of the Romantics, Poe brought into literature a new interest in the workings of the human mind. So strong was this that it made him proof against one of the weaker Romantic tendencies, that towards Primitivism. "The theorizers on Government," he said, with the Contractarian philosophers apparently in view, "who pretend always to 'begin with the beginning,' commence with Man in what they call his *natural* state—the savage. What right have they to suppose this his natural state? Man's chief idiosyncrasy being reason, it follows that his savage condition—his condition of action *without* reason—is his *unnatural* state." Like Blake, Poe assimilated Rousseau to Locke as retrograde powers. Locke of course was "America's philosopher" and his view of the mind, filtered through Reid, Stewart, and the Scottish Common Sense school, was dominant in Poe's day. Though Locke is, properly speaking, an empiricist, his immensely influential theory of knowledge . . . had become increasingly identified during the course of the eighteenth century with purely natural and rationalistic ways of thinking. Locke conceived of the mind as a blank page on which ideas of the external world were inscribed through the senses, or as a kind of mechanical organizer of sensations which were fed to it by "experience." *This view appeared very well suited to explain the processes of scientific classification* and experiment or the formation of common-sense judgements on practical matters, *but it tended to create the assumptions that only the physical, the tangible, the measurable were real,* and that consciousness was a prisoner of the senses [italics mine].

To anyone concerned with introspection and the primacy of the mind's own powers, Locke was the enemy.

In America, this diagnosis and the consequent revolt are identified with the Transcendentalists. Using James Marsh's edition (1829) of Coleridge's *Aids to Reflection,* the American Transcendentalists took over the distinction between Reason and Understanding, but they gave it a quite un-Coleridgean emphasis, an emphasis which "The Purloined Letter" shows Poe rejected. For Coleridge, with his lifelong search for unity, Reason and Understanding were complementary powers of the mind, each valuable in its own sphere which corresponded roughly to the moral and the practical. Pure Reason, for example, had no place in politics where it could only result in Jacobinism. But the moral life depended on the promptings of an intuition lying deeper than the Understanding. With the American Transcendentalists this distinction tended to harden into a frozen posture. Reason became an honorific power whose twofold purpose was to communicate with the Over-Soul and to dishonor the "sensual" Understanding. Coleridge valued the Understanding on its own terms. He rejected Godwin because he saw that "philanthropy" can't be achieved if the "homeborn" elements that insure life's continuity and allow virtue to develop—the family, for instance—are done away with. The Transcendentalists, however, were not looking for a means to *explore* reality in its various dimensions; they wanted a means to *discredit* the "sensual" Understanding. As an independent realm, to be valued for what it was, they had no interest in it. Intelligence here comes dangerously close to being freed (ambiguous word) from common experience.

In "Sonnet—To Science" we see the young Poe similarly solve the problem of the prevailing rationalistic outlook by simply rejecting it. In "The Purloined Letter," however, he tries to discern the limits of this outlook and show why it is inadequate as an account of intelligence. The interplay between the mind, the body, and experience suggests a viewpoint similar to Coleridge's and implicitly criticizes Transcendentalism. It will be recalled that the story falls into three parts. In the first G—— comes to Dupin's rooms, relates the problem, and details the steps he has already taken. Dupin listens and gives his ironic advice: "Make a thorough research of the premises." The story turns on the different ways *thorough* is understood. The second is quite short. A month has passed when G—— returns still baffled. He says he is willing to pay a reward of fifty thousand francs for the letter, whereupon Dupin tells him to draw up his cheque and produces the letter. G—— leaves and Dupin enters into a somewhat long-winded "explanation," most of which is concerned with G——'s failure as a "reasoner"; only the last couple of paragraphs treat the action by which Dupin foils D—— and recovers the letter. The interest centers in the explanation.

Why does G—— fail as a reasoner? Calling him "a functionary," Dupin says, "the remote source of his defeat lies in the supposition that the Minister is a fool, because he has acquired renown as a poet." And speaking of D——, he adds, "As poet *and* mathematician, he would reason well; as mere mathematician he could not have reasoned at all."

Clearly, the prevailing rationalistic outlook dominant in America is being criticized. Poe uses narration and dialogue to point up the restless energy of the superficial "functionary," and he contrasts this busyness with the calmer, more attractive rhythm of the reflective Dupin. Out of this comes their contrasting attitudes towards poetry. Dupin has been "guilty of certain doggerel" himself, while for G—— anyone whose interests lie that way is a "fool." Poetry, as the story reveals, though not to G——, is a form of knowledge, the necessary complement, intuitive and tending to the concrete, to mathematics, rational and tending to the abstract. As Dupin argues, both are necessary in a mutually fertilizing relationship before there is full intelligence. The rational principle cannot be divorced from intuitive perception without running the risk of reducing itself to mere cleverness. Or, we might say, a people that has no way of valuing poetry is committed to very limited ways of knowing.

G—— is committed to his "microscope"; and with this goes a certain hubris: " 'The thing is *so* plain. There is a certain amount of bulk—a space— to be accounted for in every cabinet. Then we have accurate rules. The fiftieth part of a line could not escape us.' " But somehow the letter does, ironically defining the limits of this way of thinking about the world. " 'Then we examined the house itself. We divided the entire surface into compartments, which we numbered, so that none might be missed; then we scrutinized each individual square inch throughout the premises, including the two houses immediately adjoining, with the microscope, as before.' " That "two adjoining houses" is a nice comic touch, redoubled energy serving for the lack of insight. " 'But,' " asks Dupin later, with delighted scorn, " 'what is all this boring, and probing, and sounding, and scrutinizing with the microscope, and dividing the surface of the building into registered square inches?' " Our question might well be, Why does Poe call it a microscope? He doesn't mean the familiar compound microscope, he means a magnifying glass; the thing was known and the term was present in the language for him to use (the *OED* gives 1665 for its first citation). Dupin points out that all G—— can do in an unprecedented situation is extrapolate his method, which brings more and more of the tangible (like the two adjoining houses) under review. Poe calls the glass a microscope because he wants, through this linguistic extension, to identify G——'s method with that of scientific rationalism. This outlook, as Hochfield says, "tended to create the assumptions that only the physical, the tangible, the measurable were real." The story undermines these assumptions. The immaterial or spiritual, it argues, is not only real but primary.

Dupin is a poet and the story contrasts his mode of intelligence, the imagination, with G——'s. The use of the "microscope" entails a loss of perspective, a loss, that is, of wholeness of vision. G—— is committed to a reality that is measurable only, the surface of things. The tales's central irony is that even there he cannot locate the letter, for *seeing* in this sense depends on a prior act of mind. He is cut off, in Coleridge's well-known words, from "that deep Thinking . . . attainable only by a man of deep Feeling" and locked into a Newtonian system where mind "is always passive—a lazy Looker-on on an external world." Poetry or the imagination is contrasted with the microscope; the latter divides while the former unifies. And the corresponding unity of the self in the act of knowing is its strength (just as its absence is Dupin's warrant for calling G—— "a functionary"). Poe points out the limits of the dominant American mode of thought, but he also criticizes the orthodox alternative. For Dupin is no Transcendentalist, using Reason to discredit the "sensual" Understanding, finding satisfaction in inverting the dominant view. Intelligence, properly understood, is not detached intellect; it is rooted in the life of the body and is a function of the whole person. When the tale opens Dupin and the narrator are sitting in the darkness "enjoying the twofold luxury of meditation and a meerschaum," and it is through this perspective that everything subsequent is to be seen and judged. "The high perception," as Melville was afterwards to put it, is here wedded to "the low enjoying power." Thought (or meditation: the stress falls on that ingathering that must precede activity) is from the outset of this exploration into the makeup of real intelligence intimately linked with feeling (evoked by the meerschaum), and where there is this copresence even the darkness is not prohibitive.

Poe's criticism of the impoverished sense of mind dominant in utilitarian America is not merely negative; it proceeds from a human center. American thought has customarily oscillated between unleavened materialism and unrooted idealism; but Poe's groundwork is the wholeness of the person operating through the unifying activity of the imagination. It will be useful to keep this in mind when we come to stories more wholly negative in their critique.

Poe feels disdain for the aggressive didactic rationalism of G—— but reaches a different evaluation of the narrator of "The Fall of the House of Usher" who also embodies an essential American attitude towards the mind. The distinction is a moral one, and it reminds us that Poe's social thought, *as realized in his fiction,* is more *ondoyant et divers* than the aristocratic haughtiness and contempt for the mob usually ascribed to him. Within the American tradition, from the White House down, there was widespread belief in the sufficiency of the common sense of the common man. Professor Ward has noted this paradox: "The rejection of training and experience . . . was an important aspect of nineteenth century American thought." The age was convinced that mental discipline was otiose, that real intelligence didn't need formal training, that the mind's inherent powers were adequate to any situation. Underlying this was the assumption, given spurious legitimacy by the Declaration of Independence, that the most important truths were self-evident; and the phrase "common-sense" had received a sort of sanctity from its Revolutionary association. This outlook was of course necessary for belief in the autonomous self. What Poe saw were its limitations, that in most important matters there are qualifications that can only be gained by discipline and experience, developing natural aptitude. What Lionel Trilling once called "the general import" of "The Rime of the Ancient Mariner" applies *mutatis mutandis* to "Usher"; "The world is a complex and unexpected and terrible place which is not always to be understood by the mind as we use it in our everyday tasks."

"What ails Roderick Usher?" Roy Male has asked. "That is the central question of the story." And Darrel Abel in his well-known essay adheres to this emphasis: "Five persons figure in the tale, but the interest centers exclusively in one—Roderick Usher. The narrator is uncharacterized, undescribed, even unnamed." But as usual in Poe the interest lies with the narrator. In this case he embodies the American belief in common sense, but he is taken out of the plain and simple world where this view holds easy sway and he is tested by more severe events. To focus on Roderick, fascinating as he is, is to finesse Poe's intention and meaning. And Professor Abel seems misleading when he says the narrator is uncharacterized. The opposite is true, and this characterization is a basic element in the tale.

Poe uses tone and statement to establish the narrator as the ordinary man of common sense. He is not unattractive. We see evidence of charity in his response to Usher's letter, and he has none of the hubris of Poe's swollen rationalists. But he accepts as axiomatic the adequacy of the untutored intelligence. The tale presents us with a mind incapable of the development necessary even for its own preservation. Consider the opening paragraph from the point where he first sees "the melancholy House of Usher":

> I know not how it was—but, with the first glimpse of the building, a sense of insufferable gloom pervaded my spirit. I say insufferable; for the feeling was unrelieved by any of that half-pleasurable, because poetic, sentiment with which the mind usually receives even the sternest natural images of the desolate or terrible. I looked upon the scene before me—upon the mere house, and the simple landscape features of the domain—upon the bleak walls—upon the vacant eye-like windows—upon a few rank sedges—and upon a few white trunks of decayed trees—with an utter depression of soul which I can compare to no earthy sensation more properly than to the after-dream of the reveller upon opium—the bitter lapse into every-day life—the hideous dropping off of the veil. There was an iciness, a sinking, a sickening of the heart—an unredeemed dreariness of thought which no goading of the imagination could torture into aught of the sublime.

Roderick is not around—he doesn't enter until the eighth paragraph—so this is usually allowed to provide atmosphere. But that account is exiguous, for Poe's theme, method, and the basic configuration of the tale are all outlined here. The theme emerges from the dialectical interplay between his untutored common sense and the instreaming impressions which evade it. The method emphasizes his sturdy refusal to be affected by, or quite admit the reality of, phenomena that seem to lie outside the Newtonian framework until, at the end, he directly experiences what no common sense can ever explain, no science account for.

"I know not how it was," he begins and sets out to undo that initial bafflement. The third sentence ("I looked upon the scene before me") renders the movement of his mind and conveys the reasonable tone. His eye slowly scans the scene and particular images register one-by-one on his consciousness. The adjectives provide an interesting mix of the objective— mere, simple, few, white, decayed—and the subjective—bleak, vacant eye- like, rank—and this indicates the dialectical interplay. The sentence move- ment is extraordinarily slow and clogged; words are used in combinations the tongue and lips find awkward to make in passing over from one word to the next, giving the effect of great intellectual effort, of a mind puzzled by what lies before it and pondering each successive image in hopes of making a breakthrough. This sense of a search for order (the probable sense of *poetic*) is enriched by the anaphora, which in another context might have seemed frenetic. And this is furthered by the succeeding sentence with its series of false starts ("there was an iciness, a sinking, a sickening"), implying the mind's reaching for and discarding in turn analogies which might gen- erate understanding.

The effort fails. But he is not particularly disturbed, and the paragraph pivots, so to speak: "What was it—I paused to think—what was it that so unnerved me in the contemplation of the House of Usher?" *Think* here means something like "set up a chain of reasoning"—since the preceding perceptions have not arranged themselves into any sort of order—and it is in tension with *unnerved,* which the voice naturally stresses. "It was a mystery all insoluble; nor could I grapple with the shadowy fancies that crowded upon me as I pondered." The flat monotone smothers any con- citation; whatever he might say, it is clear that he does not feel the experience as a mystery. And how much of the story is focused by that playing off of *grapple* (with its physical associations) and *fancies* (the word itself slightly dismissive)! Poe shows how the mind further smothers those "crowding fancies" by means of language which is highly abstract and undefining: "I was forced to fall back upon the unsatisfactory conclusion, that while, beyond doubt, there are combinations of very simple natural objects which have the power of thus affecting us, still the analysis of this power lies among considerations beyond our depth." How easily that is said! The undisturbed tone, his chief characteristic, continues to the end of the para- graph. But as the proleptic *mere* gives way to the experienced *shudder* after he looks into the tarn, we have the basic configuration outlined (and the ending adumbrated):

It was possible, I reflected, that a mere different arrangement of the particulars of the scene, of the details of the picture, would be sufficient to modify, or perhaps to annihilate its capacity for sorrowful impressions; and, acting upon this idea, I reined my horse to the precipitous brink of a black and lurid tarn that lay in unruffled lustre by the dwelling, and gazed down—but with a shudder even more thrilling than before—upon the remodelled and inverted images of the gray sedge, and the ghastly tree-stems, and the vacant and eye-like windows.

The next paragraph begins with a casually thrown off "Nevertheless." Nothing is going to ruffle him, but it is clear that his apparent calm is not the expression of a firm inner poise. The rest of the tale develops this theme. The narrator's tone never changes no matter how hard he has to strain to account for phenomena, and this is the key to the tale as a whole. It indicates the strength of his need to domesticate the experience and keep up the illusion that everything is explicable within the general Newtonian framework. His untutored common sense, lacking internal discipline, is unable to develop with the developing experience, and he has no other defense.

As the tale progresses, the narrator crosses the causeway, enters the house, goes deep within it to Usher's chamber, and finally—in the widely recognized analogy between House and head or brain—finds himself drawn into the recesses of Usher's mind: "It was no wonder that his condition terrified—that it infected me. I felt creeping upon me, by slow yet certain degrees, the wild influence of his own fantastic yet impressive superstitions." The OED gives "doorkeeper" for its first definition of usher, and Poe calls attention to the word in this sense: "The valet now threw open a door and ushered me into the presence of his master." This is a threshold world: having crossed the causeway the narrator leaves behind him the straightforward world of common sense; Usher opens the door on things undreamt of in the philosophies of, say, Benjamin Franklin and Ralph Waldo Emerson. The narrator's way of handling this unlooked for experience varies no more than his tone; the tone in fact is a function of a broader technique. From first to last he steadies himself by disclaimers, rational "explanations" of discordant phenomena, the cumulative effect of which is simply to undermine common sense and authenticate the experienced actuality of the final, inexplicable event. They cluster around three moments: the opening when he is trying to stave off his uneasiness, the middle when Usher recites "The Haunted Palace," and the end when he desperately casts about for ways to deny that what is happening can be. It would not be convenient to quote them all and in full context, but perhaps a sampling from the first cluster will suggest their quality. Tone as always is important; sometimes it's only a matter of a strategic "but":

> There can be no doubt that the consciousness of the rapid increase of my superstition—for why should I not so term it?

> And it might have been for this reason only.

> There grew in my mind a strange fancy—a fancy so ridiculous, indeed, that I but mention it to show the vivid force of sensations that oppressed me.

> Shaking off from my spirit what *must* have been a dream.

And so on, right down to his assigning "the work of the rushing gust" for the final opening of the door by Madeline before she crosses the ultimate threshold. We notice, however, a progressive straining in these disclaimers, seen in the emphasis given to that last *must,* with its perceptible opening of doubt.

The tension he is under is nicely realized in the long paragraph that follows Usher's recitation of his poem:

> I well remember that suggestions arising from this ballad led us into a train of thought wherein there became manifest an opinion of Usher's *which I mention not so much on account of its novelty* (for other men have thought thus), *as an account of the pertinacity with which he maintained it.* This opinion, in its general form, was that of the sentience of all vegetable things. But in his disordered fancy, the idea had assumed a more daring character, and trespassed, under certain conditions, upon the kingdom of inorganization. I lack words to express the full extent, or the earnest abandon of his persuasion. The belief, however, was connected (as I have previously hinted) with the gray stones of the home of his forefathers. The conditions of the sentience had been here, he imagined, fulfilled, in the method of collocation of these stones—in the order of their arrangement, as well as in the many fungi which overspread them, and of the decayed trees which stood around—above all, in the long undisturbed endurance of this arrangement, and in its reduplication in the still waters of the tarn. Its evidence—the evidence of the sentience—was to be seen, he said (and here I started as he spoke), in the gradual yet certain condensation of an atmosphere of their own about the

waters and the walls. The result was discoverable, he added, in that silent yet importunate and terrible influence which for centuries had moulded the destinies of his family, and which made him what I now saw him—what he was. *Such opinions need no comment, and I will make none* [italics mine].

In the paragraph a marked shift occurs. The first disclaimer is routinely made. By the end he has reached, for the only time in the tale, scorn. Why? Notice the way the third sentence from the end begins: "Its evidence—the evidence of the sentience—was to be seen, he said (and here I started as he spoke)." The key here is the phrase inside the dashes, for it gives the effect of a mind suddenly growing alert to itself and realizing what is implied by that pronoun, the intimacy with Usher's beliefs that it insinuates. The effect is a delicate one, but it seems to indicate a sudden anxious rejection of a half-acceptance of what has been said in the previous sentence. The mind, braced now and solicitous to vindicate itself, impels him to "start" as Usher continues. The closing scorn is the self-conscious expression of the alerted and braced mind. But in the whole movement across the paragraph we have an indication of the strain under which he is operating. What we are seeing, in other words, is a variety of forms of resistance, but no growth.

As the story continues his grasp weakens. He loses any precise sense of calendar time and his disclaimers grow increasingly forced. Finally the last door is opened and common sense is utterly routed. Madeline stands "without the door"; when she crosses the threshold it is to bring death. Two possibilities lie open, death or flight, and, by instinct deeper than common sense, he flies. Life is not defeated, but a certain way of regarding it most certainly is.

Poe presents two aspects of the view of mind dominant in the American tradition, neither of them adequate. Real intelligence, we see, is a matter of sensibility and it has to be able to develop from within the new and unprecedented, not restrict itself to the already known and charted. The moral dimension of Poe's art is not always recognized, but it is there. He holds no animus against the common man clinging to his common sense; he feels a certain sympathy for one whose tradition is so limited and, in the end, dangerous. But he does hold an animus against the theoretician of didactic rationalism whose arguments have determined what the common man has available to him, and who has wrongfully denied life in its depths. This moves in another direction, for such denial has important moral consequences. The American experience had given unprecedented scope to individual will: this could become unrestricted will-to-dominate when it disregarded life's moral complexity and was not controlled from below by a reverence for the mystery of the person.

The American tradition forced on Poe (as on Hawthorne and Melville) his great theme, the will-to-dominate, which is to say the will without this control operating from below and the ideal of the atomistic society forbidding rigorous control from outside. In Buber's familiar terms, the world of *It* displaced the world of *Thou,* manipulation prevailing over meeting and relationship. Poe emphasizes the cost. Other persons become looked upon not as beings to whom we are spiritually bound, but as mere objects in the external world, in short, as part of nature. The centrifugal impulse of society helped keep this obscure, but Poe seized on the hidden implications of this outlook and revealed them with prophetic insight. The will-to-dominate is, for Poe, always pathological and destructive no matter in what temperament it is expressed, and he is as quick to explore the consequences of Romantic will as of the rational didactic. The ironic structure and moral focus are turned on the narrators, romantic or rationalist, and the destructive possibilities of ideals too easily believed in are revealed.

"The Cask of Amontillado" presents a rationalist. It is a late work (1846), but it is for its clarity of development that one is tempted to call it the tale towards which all the others tended. Every word goes to characterize the narrator and at the same time to place him by moral standards of which he is insensible. The shaping irony lies in the fact that his rationalistic outlook is turned on events of a religious, indeed eschatalogical, nature. The time scheme and setting quietly enforce this. The affair with Fortunato lies fifty years in the past. Montresor was then on the bitter side of some disappointment, so he must be well into his eighties and near death as he relates his story to his Confessor ("You who so well know the nature of my soul"). Against this situation Poe rubs both Montresor's story and the attitude he takes in telling it. Like the biblical fool, in his heart he does not fear God.

He is a man obsessed with his own cleverness. In his narrative he takes particular delight in this cleverness, but, unawares, reveals its terrifying human emptiness. The carnival "madness," for example, and Fortunato tricked out in motley initially emphasize, by contrast, his cool reason. And from the first we see him plume himself on his discipline. He is a connoisseur, and his study is himself: "It must be understood, that neither by word nor deed had I given Fortunato cause to doubt my good-will. I continued, as was my wont, to smile in his face, and he did not perceive that my smile *now* was at the thought of his immolation." His view of human nature is of that type of reductive cynicism that usually goes by the name realist: "There were no attendants at home; they had absconded to make merry in honor of the time. I had told them that I should not return until the morning, and had given them explicit orders not to stir from the house. These orders were sufficient, I well knew, to insure their immediate disappearance, one and all, as soon as my back was turned." He finds something exquisite in permitting Fortunato to insist that they go on to the vaults: "Putting on a mask of black silk, and drawing a *roquelaire* closely about me, I suffered him to hurry me to my palazzo." He takes vulpine pleasure in his knowledge of what lies in wait:

"Enough," he said, "the cough is a mere nothing; it will not kill me. I shall not die of a cough."
"True—true," I replied.

And his wit enables him to triumph even over the unexpected as when Fortunato gives him a sign from freemasonry and he pulls a trowel out from within his cloak. This sense of self is obdurate and proof against *any* appeal:

"*For the love of God, Montresor!*"
"Yes," I said, "for the love of God!"

Against this, however, are two moments of inciting or prompting, their strength suggested by their being involuntary and physiological, life from out the depths protesting what the conscious mind is leading on to. These must be quelled and explained away, the grip of the rational mind reinstated. The first comes after the laying of the seventh tier. A period of silence has gone by and Montresor is curious about Fortunato's condition. He holds the torch above the opening and tries to see in: "A succession of loud and shrill screams, bursting suddenly from the throat of the chained form, seemed to thrust me violently back." Though he has consciously desired this, something in him profoundly recoils: "For a brief moment I hesitated—I trembled. Unsheathing my rapier, I began to grope with it about the recess." This, I think, is a fine psychological detail. He is using the rapier to probe the dark, fearful interior; "grope" conveys just the right sense of loss of control: "but the thought of an instant reassured me. I placed my hand upon the solid fabric of the catacombs, and felt satisfied." Here is the essence of his case. There is only the material world, the solid fabric, after all, safely there to the touch. He is restored.

The second comes in the final paragraph. No sound has succeeded his blasphemy about the love of God. Again he tries to get the torch to where he can still see in; he drops it through the tiny remaining hole and it hits the ground: "There came forth in return only a jingling of the bells." A human being has been reduced beyond language to the uncoordinated twitchings of a nervous system: "My heart grew sick—." The inciting is clear, direct—and explained away: "on account of the dampness of the catacombs." There is only the material world. Nothing else is real.

Montresor is characterized by his rationalistic outlook and haughty pride in himself. "Insult," we learn in the opening paragraph, he is far less able to bear than "injury." And it is a further point of this sense of honor that "the avenger" should "make himself felt as such to him who has done the wrong." What he wants is a certain type of feeling, a feeling of domination. This is conveyed in the paragraph that precedes the fearful moment when he is forced to draw his rapier. Soon after beginning the wall he senses, with pleasure, that Fortunato's intoxication—a barrier keeping back full recognition of his plight—has worn off: "The earliest indication I had of this was a low moaning cry from the depth of the recess. It was *not* the cry of a drunken man. There was then a long and obstinate silence. I laid the second tier, and the third, and the fourth; and then I heard the furious vibrations of the chain. The noise lasted for several minutes, during which, that I might harken to it with more satisfaction, I ceased my labors and sat down upon the bones." *Obstinate* is the key word. It indicates how badly Montresor wants to directly experience Fortunato's despair and take from that his *satisfaction*.

He is telling this as a last confession, and the irony is generated by the contrast between his rationalism pridefully centered on himself and the eschatalogical threshold he stands on. He does not feel contrition (without which there is no remission of sin) nor grasp the moral dimension of his story. For him its meaning is clear: he has had his vengeance, wreaked his will upon his enemy. The final sentence evokes his pride in his wit: "*In pace requiescat!*" "May he rest in peace!" The phrase inverts an ancient liturgical formula (just as the opening sentence inverts a proverb); in doing so it completes Poe's meaning. The Latin Mass said in Poe's time ordinarily ended with the priest turning to the congregation and giving it his parting blessing, followed by the words, "*Ite missa est*"— "Go, the mass is ended." The only exception was the Mass for the Dead. In this there was no blessing; the priest simply turned and expressed the hope of the faithful: "*Requiescat in pace.*" Montresor's words are reflexive in their meaning, a point Poe underscores by inverting them. The ending cooperates in the placing of his moral obtuseness; it is he who has been dead in his humanity these fifty years.

Though there are still those who cherish the belief that "Ligeia" is about a woman who comes back from the dead through the agency of her will and another woman's body, the interpretation first developed by Roy P. Basler makes a response relevant to what Poe is offering. "Ligeia" shows "the power of frustrate love to create an erotic symbolism and mythology in compensation for sensual disappointment." There is of course no Ligeia; she is wholly the creation of the narrator's fantasy, the product of an erotomania rooted, I would guess, in a habit of masturbation. The account given by Joel Porte is more or less accurate, but his judgment—"The vitality of the world of dreams is the true underlying theme"—is quite wrong, if only by one word. It is the power, not the vitality, of the world of dreams that is demonstrated, for the theme has to do with the way a diseased fantasy is the enemy of life. Like Monstresor, the narrator here works his will upon another human being without any feeling for what he is doing; he is incapable of any living response to the individual and unique.

W. H. Auden has said somewhere that the tendency of the Romantic hero was to want to be God, and this story provides a case where the generalization actually applies. The story is quite simple and has a simple structure; there is a Ligeia-half and a Rowena-half. The first part is a fantasy; in the second part fantasy impinges on the real world with terrifying results. Poe uses the dark-heroine / light-heroine contrast and a marked shift in style to help establish the differences. The narrator, through Ligeia, experiences himself as worshipped ("idolatry" is a conspicuous word whenever his attention is directed towards her) in and through sexual passion. His response, in his throes, is to believe himself coming close to some ultimate knowledge, only to lose it. This knowledge is occasioned by Ligeia's eyes in moments of intense passion (Poe's pun could hardly be more pointed), and it called a "sentiment" which he "feels." The key to the tale is the quote from Glanvill used as its epigraph. This is introduced by the narrator, not Ligeia, and he avers that it "never failed to inspire me with the sentiment": " 'And the will therein lieth, which dieth not. Who knoweth the mysteries of the will with its vigor? For God is but a great will pervading all things by nature of its intentness. Man doth not yield himself to the angels, nor unto death utterly, save only through the weakness of his feeble will.' " The will which operates is his, though he wants us to believe it is hers. If Ligeia, being all that she is, worships him, what must he be? And she will come back from the dead to go on worshipping him!

In the second half the narrator marries the real person, Lady Rowena Travanion of Tremaine, probably thinking his sexual fantasies can be realized in the world of actual experience. The marriage chamber, at any rate, is arranged to that end:

> But in the draping of the apartment lay, alas! the chief phantasy of all. . . . The material was the richest cloth of gold. It was spotted all over, at irregular intervals, with arabesque figures, about a foot in diameter, and wrought upon the cloth in patterns of the most jetty black. But these figures partook of the true character of the arabesque only when regarded from a single point of view. By a contrivance now common, and indeed traceable to a very remote period of antiquity, they were made changeable in aspect. To one entering the room, they bore the appearance of simple monstrosities; but upon a farther advance, this appearance gradually departed; and step by step, as the visitor moved his station in the chamber, he saw himself surrounded by an endless succession of the ghastly forms which belong to the superstition of the Norman, or arise in the guilty slumbers of the monk. The phantasmagoric effect was vastly heightened by the artificial introduction of a strong continual current of wind behind the draperies—giving a hideous and uneasy animation to the whole.

What this seems to mean is that the draperies were decorated with figures that were lewd and which, by the air-current device, could be animated so as to become pornographic. Rowena recoils from her fate, but he finds a temporary pleasure in sexual cruelty: "That my wife dreaded the fierce moodiness of my temper—that she shunned me and loved me but little— I could not help perceiving; but it gave me rather pleasure than otherwise. I loathed her with a hatred belonging more to demon than to man." She experiences deep psychological anguish, while he finds himself reverting more and more to the fantast's world where the will meets no resistances. After a period she begins to decline physically—everything in this world is destructive of vitality—and he poisons her to hasten her along. His desire is to experience the climactic triumph of his fantasy. And so in the famous final paragraph he believes Ligeia is coming back through Rowena's corpse to continue her idolatry to him.

Poe's theme is a moral one: the triumph of fantasy is destructive of actual living with its demands. Rowena is not met with in the world of relationship; she is used by the narrator for his enjoyment in the world of *It*. Like Montresor, he is an imperious, autonomous self for whom others are atomistic objects to be manipulated. For them the will is neither disciplined by a sense of complexity nor controlled from below by a feeling for the mystery of the person. In each case this has consequences for the body. Speaking of "the Romantic retreat from the physical," John Fraser has noted that "the body has been suspect much of the time in American literature, perhaps because it is the body that most ineluctably sets limits to individual human ambitions." These narrators, caught in the grip of a will-to-dominate, recognize no such limits while yet insisting on their own virtue. That situation mirrors in its way what has sometimes been called the irony of American history.

Poe's tales explore, as fiction can, the moral consequences of those ideals and values, and consequent habits of thought and feeling, that formed the American tradition. His limited but real achievement was to reveal, however obliquely, the human consequences of the tradition, to cut through the fogbank of optimism and insist on its destructive potential. Unlike Cooper, Hawthorne, and Melville, he saw little to celebrate in the American experience and his work is almost wholly negative in expression and impact. That is why, perhaps, he spent so much of himself, at the last, constructing the aesthetico-cosmology that arches back to the poetry of withdrawal of the Romantic anchorite. In the end he could not, alone, sustain the necessary tension. There is a sense in which American society defeated him. But not before he had taken its measure.

Poe: Writing and the Unconscious

Gregory S. Jay

> Can the dispossession of consciousness to the profit of another home of
> meaning be understood as an act of reflection, as the first gesture of
> reappropriation?
>
> RICOEUR, *Freud and Philosophy*

> But human megalomania will have suffered its third and most wounding
> blow from the psychological research of the present time which seeks to prove
> to the ego that it is not even master of its own house, but must content itself
> with scanty information of what is going on unconsciously in its mind. We
> psychoanalysts were not the first and not the only ones to utter this call to
> introspection.
>
> FREUD, *Introductory Lectures on Psychoanalysis*

> But evil things, in robes of sorrow,
>   Assailed the monarch's high estate . . .
> And, round about his home, the glory
>   That blushed and bloomed
> Is but a dim-remembered story
>   Of the old time entombed.
>
> "The Haunted Palace"

Contemporary critical theory has most insistently haunted two related
structures: Romantic literature since Blake, and philosophy after Locke.
Some have argued that all "modern" writing should be defined by its
response to the Romantics; in philosophy, most particularly on the Con-
tinent, it is Kant and Hegel who serve as the commanding centers from

From *The American Renaissance: New Dimensions* 28, no. 1 (1983). © 1983 by Associated University Presses, Inc.

which others try to depart. Thus we should not be surprised that post-structuralist criticism finds Edgar Allan Poe so amiable a subject, for Poe's chief struggle was his attempt to emerge, as a writer and a thinker, from the influential shadow cast by Romantic poetry and Idealist philosophy (German and American). With the aid of recent theorists, we may better understand what Edward H. Davidson asserted in his pioneering study: "that Poe was a 'crisis' in the Romantic and the symbolic imagination. He came near the end (if such directions have 'beginning' and 'end') of the idealist or Romantic expression and mind." But Davidson's formula sounds too passive, however fated Poe's inherited dilemmas may be. Though from "Tamerlane" to *Eureka* Poe's tests show a desire to recover the Ideal, the True, and the Beautiful, his stories and poems and essays constantly repeat a pattern of aggression against the Transcendental. The increasing number of confessional tales, in fact, suggests a compulsive need to confess a kind of "guilt" for the "murder" of what is elsewhere lamented as lost.

The mental flights, reflections, and ratiocinations of Poe's protagonists yield not only this guilt but a related dissolution of self and identity. The horrible results of Poe's ecstatic states upset the Romantic commonplace that proposes an access to the divine through abnormal states of consciousness. Often his narrators seem condemned by genealogy to extraordinary speculations. "I am," writes William Wilson (but which one?), "the descendent of a race whose imaginative and easily excitable temperament has at all times rendered them remarkable." In Wilson's case, introspection produces a doppelgänger who becomes a mortal antagonist. Murder or revenge is regularly carried out against doubles of the self in Poe ("Loss of Breath," "Metzengerstein," "The Tell-Tale Heart," "The Purloined Letter," "The Imp of the Perverse," "The Cask of Amontillado"), as well as against the bodies of those women conventionally symbolizing Sublime Knowledge. "The essential Poe fable," observes Michael Davitt Bell, "however elaborately the impulse may be displaced onto a double or a lover, is a tale of compulsive self-murder." Bell's interpretation of this "murder" as primarily a symbolic destruction of the sexual or sensual self, however, misses the important conjunction of sexuality, philosophy, and textuality in Poe's works.

The dethronement of the self's monarchy by the irruptions of buried passions does signify at the sexual level, to be sure; yet this upheaval represents at another level only one example of the general crisis of self and identity as philosophical concepts, or as viable notions for the writer. The Romantic/Hegelian/Transcendental placement of the self at the center of philosophy's union with Beauty, Spirit, or the Over-Soul makes of coherent personal identity a prerequisite to Truth itself. As the writer's character or identity, be he philosopher or poet, proceeds from that of the text, the Truth of writing becomes susceptible to a double assault. First, there are elements in the text that repeat those of other texts, thus threatening the dream of original identity (Poe's purloinings from other writers are notorious). This fear we find in Poe's obsessions with the burdens of family inheritance and the problems of discerning plagiarism, both of which raise questions about the relationships between creativity and repetition. Second, there are parts of the self that seem not its own, residing in an unconscious which, like Poe's many ancestral mansions, houses the decaying but persistent recollections of an influential past. To bemoan inheritance, rail against plagiarism, or entomb one's double is to seek an exclusion of the other who shadows identity. In so often exposing Truth as a deceptive effect of violence or revisionary experience, Poe finds (often in horror) that fissure which ultimately destroys the Romantic and Idealist structures of reflection he so perversely inhabits and haunts.

Whether "seriously" or "parodically," in "Ligeia" or "How to Write a Blackwood Article," Poe repeatedly employs the language, plots, symbols, and ideas that are his legacy from Gothic fiction, British poetry, and German metaphysics. To read Poe is to interpret the significance of his rearrangements of these family estates. They are undone from within, either by the return of the repressed other or by a hyperbolic mockery of the visionary's pretensions. In both his "arabesques" and "grotesques," Poe's method may aptly be compared to Jacques Derrida's definition of "deconstruction" as "inhabiting" structures "*in a certain way . . .* borrowing all the strategic and economic resources of subversion from the old structure." The subsequent reappropriation results, not in a new mastery of Truth (which is what Dupin would like us to believe), but in an edifying collapse of both terms in the dualism (true/false, construction/deconstruction, self/other, etc.). Like the "House of Usher" and its narrator, deconstructive reflection "always in a certain way falls prey to its own work."

This is to say that a deconstruction of Truth cannot itself be "true" in the old sense. It becomes rather, as in Poe's deployment of his literary borrowings, a rhetoric of signifying effects. Here we recall Poe's aesthetic principle that poetry "has no concern with Duty or with Truth." Without that concern, however, and the desires it engenders, Poe's work is inexplicable. He ceaselessly explores the imagination's power to know the "Supernal Loveliness." Poe's critique of Truth's place in the imagination's work displaces the center of Romantic and philosophical discourse, but strategically that displacement (or "murder") serves as prelude to the appearance of an idea of Beauty that functions in much the same structuring way as Truth once had. Yet Truth is not Beautiful in Poe, or vice versa. The insistent conclusion, contradicting the lingering transcendentalism of Poe's optative moods, is that the "death" of Truth which is the prerequisite of ideal beauty cannot be dialectically resolved. As Joseph N. Riddel has argued, the presence of Beauty remains contaminated by the confession of its fatal means of production. The same holds true for the identity of a self produced by the "murder" of the Other. In either case, we end up in a world where both truth and self are rhetorical effects, and, as such, vulnerable to the unsettlings of identity that language and interpretation always fall prey to.

I

Poe's journeys into the disestablishment of inherited constructs are subversive versions of standard Romantic themes. For his own purposes he took up the Romantic reaction against empiricism and "common sense" philosophy. In "How to Write a Blackwood Article," Blackwood advises the Signora Psyche Zenobia: "Be sure and abuse a man called Locke." Northrop Frye made "The Case against Locke" his opening explanation of Blake's romanticism, and Robert Langbaum begins with Wordsworth's reaction to Locke in his own fine account of literature and identity. The Romantic critique of rational reflection included a general, but variously imagined, substitution of perception for reasoning. Higher, even divine, truths might be approached by a visionary experience whose significant prerequisite is the initial dissolution or making-absent of mundane sensory realities. The list of such enabling experiences is lengthy, and most appear in Poe (e.g., childhood, drugs, dreams, liquor, art work, books, moonlight, remembrance, sleeplessness, mesmerism, sea voyages, madness). The exemplary passages are in Wordsworth, for there the distinct necessity of overthrowing the "absolute dominion" of the "bodily eye," and of replacing it with the creative "recollection," is most clearly articulated. When "the light of sense / Goes out," the "invisible world" stands revealed, though in an aspect more heartening than the terror-inspiring apparitions of the recalled Ligeia or Madeline Usher. Emerson gives the American version in *Nature*'s chapter on "Idealism," a text Poe could hardly not have read:

> If the Reason be stimulated to more earnest vision, outlines and surfaces become transparent, and are no longer seen; causes and spirits are seen through them. The best moments of life are these delicious awakenings of the higher powers, and the reverential withdrawing of nature before its God.

"As a matter of fact," wrote Hegel, "thinking is always the negation of what we have immediately before us."

The recurrent narrative pattern in Poe takes us along with a protagonist on just such an extraordinary voyage of visionary negation, borrowing this structure in a way usually both sympathetic to its aspirations and critical of its results. Example after example could be adduced to demonstrate how such arabesque *rites de passage* work in Poe, not simply as "excuses" for the "supernatural," but as critical variations wrought consciously on the tradition. Even Dupin's ratiocination, which in the trajectory of Poe's career is entertained as a possible substitute for and improvement on the visionary, becomes a double of hypnosis: "I cannot better explain my meaning," says Vankirk in "Mesmeric Revelation," speaking of his insights into God and immortality, "than by the hypothesis that the mesmeric exaltation enables me to perceive a train of ratiocination." In "The Imp of the Perverse," Poe drops such devices of artificial exaltation, positing our impulse to throw ourselves into the "abyss" as a fatal law of character admitting of "no intelligible principle." But such a defensive abstraction of motive comes late in the career, after countless passages like the following from "Berenice":

> My baptismal name is Egaeus; that of my family I will not mention. Yet there are no towers in the land more time-honored than my gloomy, gray, hereditary halls. Our line has been called a race of visionaries; and in many striking particulars—in the character of the family mansion—in the frescoes of the chief saloon—in the tapestries of the dormitories—in the chiselling of some buttresses in the armory—but more especially in the gallery of antique paintings—in the fashion of the library chamber—and, lastly, in the very peculiar nature of the library's contents, there is more than sufficient evidence to warrant the belief.
>
> The recollections of my earliest years are connected with that chamber, and with its volumes—of which latter I will say no more. Here died my mother. Herein was I born. . . . Thus awakening from the long night of what seemed, but was not, nonentity, at once into the very regions of fairy-land—into a palace of imagination—into the wild dominions of monastic thought and erudition—it is not singular that I gazed around me with a startled and ardent eye—that I loitered away my boyhood in books, and dissipated my youth in reverie; but it *is* singular that as years rolled away, and the noon of manhood found me

still in the mansion of my fathers—it *is* wonderful what stagnation there fell upon the springs of my life—wonderful how total an inversion took place in the character of my commonest thought. The realities of the world affected me as visions, and as visions only, while the wild ideas of the land of dreams became, in turn,—not the material of my everyday existence—but in very deed that existence utterly and solely in itself.

Like Usher and Dupin, Egaeus's home is the library. He is a place where other writings meet, less a soul than an intertextual confluence. His identity, and that of Poe's work, appears to be that of a shadow cast by others. Egaeus's "anxiety of influence" (Harold Bloom's term) so holds him that the "noon of manhood" finds him still in the mansion of his forefathers, an edifice of historicism as well as textuality. The predicament afflicts many of Poe's narrators, for the intertextuality of his creations necessarily involves the danger of unoriginality. The significant twist here is in the result of Egaeus's "inversion" of "everyday existence." This making-absent of the mundane world and its replacement with the "wild ideas of the land of dreams" takes him backward into repeating the characteristics of the past, and of his fathers. Poe draws a structural parallel between a personal and a literary or cultural unconscious. Egaeus's "wild dreams" will represent, in good Freudian fashion, the conflicts and desires of his individual unconscious, thus disrupting his coherent identity with impulses from elsewhere that he (the idea of the unified self) does not author. At the level of writing or culture, we are likewise born into a context of influences; when we come to consciousness of ourselves as individuals, we do so always already through the categories and axioms we have inherited. The poetic "anxiety of influence," so evident in Poe's Romantic protagonists and in his own responses to Coleridge, Byron, Wordsworth, and Shelley, is only a local manifestation of that general tension between traditions and individual talents that shapes cultural history as a whole. Thus the "ancestral mansions" and genealogical systems in Poe's work represent the machinery of inheritance in the largest sense, and inform, as we shall later see, Poe's dark criticism of the contemporary American rage for the idealism of literary and national "self-reliance." Genealogy becomes the aptest structural metaphor because of its theoretical and historical strengths as a system for denominating and regulating the passage of identity, authority, and property through the mutability of time. It is no accident that so many of Poe's transcendental seekers of Truth are aristocrats. Poe's attraction to the hierarchies of aristocracy is one with his temptation toward the Transcendental, but both fall victim to the discovery of the work of the unconscious and the other, those bastards and outcasts whose exclusion enables the system, and who cannot forever be denied the recognition of their kinship.

Egaeus begins as a version of the "belated" Romantic mind. Berenice's disease (which like those afflicting his other heroines appears to result from no intelligible principle) coincides with a drastic change in his imagination, with ghoulish results. The distinction Egaeus uses to explain how he comes to rip the teeth from the prematurely buried Berenice concerns the difference between the "attentive" and the "speculative" imaginations. The latter he inherits; the former is the "disease" he falls into when Berenice grows ill. The "attentive" fixes on "frivolous" objects of contemplation, such as the "device on the margin, or in the typography of a book." His reveries sometimes involved the "frequent repetition" of a word until it ceased to convey any idea whatever ("Quoth the Raven, 'Nevermore' "?). He hopes to banish the words of the fathers and to transcend their influence. Berenice's fatal illness seems to cause Egaeus's mental derangement, or to enable his effort to dissolve everyday reality. In fact, his disease comes immediately after her spells of epilepsy, trancelike states resembling "positive dissolution" and ending in an abrupt return to life. The same pattern holds for the workings of the "attentive" faculty. Unlike the "speculative," it could not transcend objects, but "pertinaciously returning in upon the original objects as a centre," remained fixated to the world, the body of the other.

His previous attitude toward Berenice—"not as a being of the earth, earthy, but as the abstraction of such a being"—was a "speculation" now diseased by an interior malady, an irruption of the other within the self. For Egaeus, her illness is the insistent return of what had been repressed, her "earthy" self, and his own mortality. What drives him mad as he watches her die is "the singular and most appalling distortion of her personal identity." Thus the "death" of his betrothed occasions his ghastly attempt to assert her immortality by wresting her symbolically pure white teeth from the grave. The horrible paradox governing him is this: the desire for immortal identity runs into a fatal conflict with the immortal identities of others; to "murder" or "repress" those others in the service of one's own identity involves an intense attention to them as objects, and a repetition of them in reflection that subsequently leaves a resistent trace of the other in the dream of originality. Berenice's premature burial makes Egaeus's perverse attempt to transcend mutability possible, but her teeth remain signs both of the body and of Egaeus's own repressed fears. Her mouth signifies (as others have noted) a displaced *vagina dentata*. It resembles other "abysses" in Poe, a negative version of transcendental aspiration. The self leaps into an unconscious beyond that it cannot control, but which beckons with its secret script.

Poe's inquiry into the instability of personal identity shapes much of his work. A variety of topics serve as its vehicle, including metempsychosis, reincarnation, doppelgängers, and spiritual immortality. The interest is especially obvious and keen in the earlier tales and poems written most immediately under the influence of Poe's reading in Gothic fiction, British poetry, and Idealist philosophy. In "Morella," a tale of the transmigration of soul from mother to daughter, the narrator-husband-father tells us of Morella's "profound" "erudition" in the "mystical writings" of the "early German literature." Meeting her "by accident," his soul "burned with fires it had never before known; but the fires were not of Eros." He finds "tormenting" the "unusual meaning" and "vague intensity" of his passions. Since Poe's epigraph comes from Plato's *Symposium*, we can assume that "Eros" here means a sublimating Platonic love that leads to the Divine, and that the narrator begins by repressing the explicitly physical aspect of his attraction to Morella's person. But in his daughter's figure she returns, and he "shuddered at its too perfect *identity*" with Morella's.

Morella's "disquisitions" in "theological morality" cited "above all, the doctrines of *Identity* as urged by Schelling." The narrator summarizes:

> That identity which is termed personal, Mr. Locke, I think, truly defines to consist in the sameness of a rational being. And since by person we understand an intelligent essence having reason, and since there is a consciousness which always accompanies thinking, it is this which makes us all to be that which we call *ourselves*—thereby distinguishing us from other beings that think, and giving us our personal identity. But the *principium individuationis*—the notion of that identity *which at death is or is not lost forever*, was to me—at times, a consideration of intense interest; not more from the perplexing and exciting nature of its consequences, than from the marked and agitated manner in which Morella mentioned them.

Morella's "marked and agitated manner" captivates the narrator. The troubled sublimity of her appearance inspires the arabesque or elevating experience that precipitates him into disaster. Her "manner" is her style, and thus she embodies that "mesmerism" of language Poe finds typical of Romantic literature and German philosophy.

The prospect of immortality, of the repetition of characters, oppresses rather than exalts the narrator's soul: "Shall I then say that I longed with an earnest and consuming desire for the moment of Morella's decease?'' The syntax indicates her "decease" as a substitute for coitus. The more she talked of spiritual immortality, the more his repressed desires were thwarted, as she divorces body from soul in quest of eternal identity. Her death would put an end to his desire and prepare them for a spiritual union in death (that embrace in the tomb found from "The Visionary" to "Annabel Lee"). So her eyes become especially repugnant: "my soul sickened and became giddy with the giddiness of one who gazes downward into some dreary and unfathomable abyss." His lust for her death is perverse, a fascination with what the abyss will reveal, even at the cost of that bodily organ that stands for the self. Those eyes, as Daniel Hoffmann has argued, are displaced vaginas again, "her meaning eyes" inviting a glimpse into his own carnal nature, his place in a temporal order of determined creations. Like the lakes and tarns throughout Poe's writings, those eyes are revisions into the Romantic topos of the reflective pool, whose spring waters flow from the pond of Narcissus. The association of abyss, eye, and lake in Poe suggests the abysmal quality of self-reflection, as the view into the beyond gives back not a heightened vision of one's true self but a bottomless speculation on the otherness we find there.

Morella's gradual reappearance in her daughter is, like the death of Rowena in "Ligeia," a barely disguised wish fulfillment of the narrator's. He perversely christens his daughter with the dead woman's name: "What prompted me then, to disturb the memory of the dead? What demon urged me to breathe that sound? What fiend spoke from the recesses of my soul?" Morella's transmigration turns into an allegory of the voice of the narrator's repetition compulsion. The repetition compulsion is Freud's coinage for the unconscious reenactment in the present of ideas, relationships, or traumas from the past. The present self is literally made an actor in a drama authored by another, in this case the unconscious. Freud once hoped that such repetition might be worked over into remembrance, a revision that masters repetition and establishes the power of present narratives over past plots. In practice, the issue became "metapsychological" when Freud attempted to explain the repetition of unpleasurable experiences. He argued that Erotic desire went beyond the pleasure principle in that its reproductive functions lead to change, rather than to the restoration of a past state. The repression enabling Freud's Eros, however, is his exclusion of a human situation by the use of a biological tropology of "germ cells." This allowed him to make absent the most prominent and forbidding repetition compulsion in Freudian sexuality: the imagining of the sexual act as a return to the mother. The narrator in "Morella" likewise hopes to cure and master repetition by recalling Morella's name, but what occurs instead is the involuntary dramatization of his own entrapment in a past fixation. For him, horror is redoubled when his original trauma before Morella's person and style is repeated with his daughter's transformation. The eternal identity of Morella turns into the terror of the past's tyranny over the present. The return of the repressed is immortality's dark double. The narrator's own identity comes undone as the repetition compulsion commands him to enact the script of the unconscious. The narrative text repeats the process, characteristically shrouding its content in a host of protestations of incomprehension and vagueness. The use of a first-person narrative, or of a nameless observer-double, allows Poe's texts to perform the discourse of a self beside itself, a layering of "secret writings." It challenges our notions of authorship and reading. We are prompted to interpret this discourse of the other that haunts the mystified accounts of these men driven to commit and confess acts for which their disturbed consciousness can ostensibly find no intelligible principle. We are tempted to become like Dupin, trying to restore the letter to its proper home.

The problem of identity in "Morella" comes out of Poe's reading in Locke's "Of Identity and Diversity," from *An Essay concerning Human Understanding*. Locke initially defines the "principium Individuationis" as spatio-temporal noncontradiction, "It being impossible for two things of the same kind, to be or exist in the same instant, in the very same place; or one and the same thing in different places." This is obviously not the case with such identities as Ligeia or William Wilson. Locke argues that if we define "identity of Man" as "one Organization of Life in several successively fleeting Particles of Matter," then we shall "find it hard, to make an *Embryo*, one of *Years*, mad, and sober, the same Man, by any Supposition that will not make it possible for *Seth, Ismael, Socrates, Pilate, St. Austin,* and *Caesar Borgia* to be the same man." If we allow "the identity of Soul alone" to make "the same Man," then we fall into "the Notions of those Philosophers, who allow of Transmigration." As the latter would considerably confuse the Last Judgment, Locke sets out to redefine the relation between "*Personal Identity*" and the "*Idea of a Man*."

In the passage Poe paraphrases in "Morella," Locke reduces the identity of man to a "self" that is noncontradictory, ever-present consciousness, without the play of unconscious forces: "When we see, hear, smell, taste, feel, meditate, or will any thing, we know that we do so." So much for the "imp of the perverse," and for all those Poe protagonists driven by "no intelligible principle":

For since consciousness always accompanies thinking, and 'tis that, that makes every one to be, what he calls *self*; and thereby distinguishes himself from all other thinking things, in this alone consists *Personal Identity*, i.e. the sameness of a rational Being; And as far as this consciousness can be extended backwards to any past Action or Thought, so far reaches the Identity of that *Person*; it is the same *self* now it was then; and 'tis by the same *self* with this present one that now reflects on it, that the Action was done.

It is this equation of self with a reflective consciousness both immediate and recollective that Poe's texts turn into an oddity. Even Locke recognizes the times of heterogeneity in consciousness: forgetfulness, intoxication, the instances "when we say such an one *is not himself,* or is *besides himself.*" This unhappy anomaly he solves by simply excluding these fits of otherness from personal identity:

If there be any part of its [the self's] Existence, which I cannot upon recollection join with that present consciousness, whereby I am now my *self,* it is in that part of its Existence no more my *self,* than any other immaterial Being. For whatsoever any Substance has thought or done, which I cannot recollect, and by my consciousness make my own Thought and Action, it will no more belong to me, whether a part of me thought or did it, than if it had been thought or done by any other immaterial Being any where existing.

This self is a self-discourse, an uninterrupted narrative that excludes anything violating the control of its self-representations. Locke's "self" defends against the influence of others, against thoughts or acts it cannot "own" and which do not "belong" to it. We are not surprised that Locke was the founding philosopher of "private property." Locke's self only feels at home in a discourse or consciousness that owns and disposes of its properties, and which is *essentially* not identifiable with anything or anyone outside the boundaries of its authorized entitlements. The ordeals of Poe's narrators tell us much about the fallacy of equating "self" and "self-consciousness." Morella's "immortality" can be read as the action of the narrator's unconscious, and thus as a critique of the "principium Individuationis" supposedly demonstrated by Morella's transmigration. His horror at her return is a fearful response to the "immortality" of an alien part of himself.

The plot of "Morella" is typical of Poe in that the death of a beautiful woman is the enabling device that occasions the narrator's excursion into visionary consciousness. The unmaking of his identity that follows proceeds in part from his implicit wish fulfillment, his "guilt" for her death. This guilt is often obscured by a displacement into lament and adolescent melancholy, or occluded by a rhetoric of arabesque frenzy. An example of the latter is in "Ligeia," when the narrator's evident poisoning of Rowena (to enable the "return" of the transcendentalist Ligeia) is presented as an opium dream of terror, in which the "angelic aspect" of Ligeia commits the fatal act. He has already cast Rowena into her "sudden illness" by surrounding her with the arabesque furnishings whose effect is the negation of mundane reality (Rowena's body). The guilt of these men grows more explicit in Poe's career, into "The Fall of the House of Usher" and "The Black Cat." The lament for the lost lady increasingly becomes the hysterical confession of her willful entombment, or, in the poems, the delightful expression of necrophilia, as in "For Annie": "And I lie so composedly, / Now, in my bed, / (Knowing her love) / that you fancy me dead—." The composing of Poe's writings into confessional narratives includes his stories of revenge, of doubles murdered in an allegory of adultery and self-destruction. To understand these developments, we need to turn to the source of Poe's dead ladies, and to the strange adaptation of this plot to Poe's theory of poetry.

II

Poe's war on plagiarism and his lifting of materials from other writers turned to his own purposes an early anxiety of influence experienced under the spell of Coleridge and Byron. A wealth of criticism has disinterred many of Poe's sources, but none have followed Floyd Stovall's passing insight that Poe's "effort to be original" stirred a fanatic attempt "to eradicate all traces of influence" in his poetry. For my purposes, the key poet here is Byron, and the central text his *Manfred*. It provides Poe with many of his stock Romantic devices, including of course the Byronic hero and the dead lady, as well as a simoon, ominous red lights, and a confession narrative. More importantly, Manfred's tale, as Poe reads it, becomes the story of the end of Romantic and philosophical idealism.

Manfred's achievement of Transcendental knowledge is haunted by his mournful remembrance of the dead Astarte. In an "all-nameless hour" he knew her, and in that climax of his quest his "embrace was fatal." Manfred's double ("She was like me in lineaments"), Astarte dies ostensibly as a result of his Satanic, Faustian ambition: "The Tree of Knowledge is not that of

Life." Doubtless Poe fixed on *Manfred* partly because his unconscious felt guilty for his own mother's death. His descriptions of Ligeia, Usher, and others mingle his own features with hers, as in mourning he introjectively identifies with her to "immortalize" her. His ambivalent violence toward such composite figures expresses the tension between self-punishing guilt and a desire for revenge against her for abandoning him as she dies into a spiritual world.

"I loved her, and destroy'd her," wails Manfred. The implicit narcissism of his love, coupled with his otherworldly loneliness, suggests that the search for self-mastery may end in self-murder and an exclusion of the other. Unable to demolish consciousness in forgetfulness or oblivion, he has Astarte conjured up, to ask her forgiveness. She instead pronounces his doom, which works a curious effect on Manfred:

> If that I did not know philosophy
> To be of all our vanities the motliest,
> The merest word that ever fooled the ear
> From out the schoolman's jargon, I should deem
> The golden secret, the sought "Kalon," found,
> And seated in my soul.
>
> (3.1.9–14)

The apparition of the dead, accusing Astarte brings a calm and truth the living lady never inspired. And yet that "If" casts doubt upon this ascension-through-death. His secure sense of guilt empowers at the end his resistance to the demons and his declaration that "The mind which is immortal makes itself / Requital for its good or evil thoughts,— / Is its own origin of ill and end." This psychologizing of his fate turns guilt into the vehicle of truth and the self's identity. In his "crime," in the destruction of the apparently desirable presence, Manfred makes his vision of the "sought 'Kalon,' found." In Manfred's guilt the Romantic dousing of the light of sense becomes the murder of the beautiful lady. The absence of the world, and of its transcendental center, is the precondition of Manfred's self and heroic text. The poem unfolds as the structure of his compulsive remembrance, until Manfred returns to the tower where they loved and she died, much as Poe and his Psyche will unconsciously find themselves suddenly at the tomb of the lost Ulalume. Writing withdraws from immediate presence, displaces what is before it, eclipses (if it can) the old gods, and leaves the trace of a "guilt" for the necessary "murder" of former truths and texts.

In "Byron and Miss Chaworth," Poe explicitly describes the advantages for the poetic imagination in the lady's absence. Although he acknowledges Miss Chaworth's charms, Poe concludes that it was "better" that "their intercourse was broken up in early life and never uninterruptedly resumed in after years":

> If she responded at all, it was merely because the necromancy of *his* words of fire could not do otherwise than exhort a response. In absence, the bard bore easily with him all the fancies which were the basis of his flame—a flame which absence itself but served to keep in vigor. . . . She to him was the Egeria of his dreams—the Venus Aphrodite that sprang, in full and supernal loveliness, from the bright foam upon the storm-tormented ocean of his thoughts.

This affirmation of the Romantic visionary formula hardly seems applicable to the horrific figures of Poe's uncharneled ladies. An axiom like "I could not love except where Death / Was mingling his with Beauty's breath" suggests the poet felt threatened by the lady's presence. An "overdetermined" signifier, Poe's lady stands variously and often simultaneously for: (1) the body, which the lady's presence excites, thus awakening the unconscious work of the instinctive other within the rational man; (2) the cultural inheritance (familial, national, European), which forms an influential other in the mind that dictates to the self; (3) truth as a metaphysical absolute; (4) the truths and beauties of past authors. If "supernal loveliness" requires the "death" of the other, then the ideals of truth, self, or originality depend on a repeated attention to what they seem to exclude. The same applies to the poet's revisions (or "murders") of his precursors. In fact, "supernal Loveliness" is also the term Poe uses in "The Poetic Principle" for that transcendent Beauty poetry vainly aspires to. The "most entrancing" of "poetic moods" doesn't follow the "brief and indeterminate glimpses" of Beauty, but rather from the "petulant, impatient sorrow at our inability to grasp *now,* wholly, here on earth, at once and for ever," a "portion of that Loveliness." In other words, no past poet could have precluded this poet's vision; and besides, failure to transcend now inspires the best poetry.

In the preface to his first volume of poetry, the "Letter to B——," Poe attacks Wordsworth and Coleridge (though he ends by stealing, almost verbatim, the latter's definition of poetry). "He belittles their poetry," writes Stovall, "in order to persuade the reader that it has not influenced his own." Poe joins the debate over the American writer's originality in reference to the "established wit of the world . . . for it is with literature as with law or empire—an established name is an estate in tenure, or a throne in possession." Disparaging Wordsworth's supposed didacticism,

Poe states, "He seems to think that the end of poetry is, or should be, instruction—yet it is a truism that the end of our existence is happiness." The removal of truth from the center of writing, and its replacement by "effect" (the correlative of arabesque elevations like opium or mesmerism) makes for a poetics that disorders logocentric structures such as genealogy or poetic tradition. Writing without such truth is the rhetoric of effects, and it throws us into a speculative abyss wherein we witness the disestablishment of "proper" forms and meanings. The maelstrom, the arabesquely furnished apartment, Dupin's library—these and other such derangements of "reality" are analogous to the space of writing itself, which likewise affects us in substituting its representations for our "normal" presences. The hysterical confession is also such a state, a literary form exemplifying how the telling of truth and the discourse of the other double one another. These spaces of representation provide the same perverse opportunities as those dark reflective waters that often occupy the center in Poe's poems and tales. They form a shadowy critical mirror of that idealism Poe sometimes indulged. In the review of Drake and Halleck, Poe extolls "that evergreen and radiant Paradise, which the true poet knows, and knows alone, as the limited realm of his authority—as the circumscribed Eden of his dreams." Yet we find far different scenes in his work from the pastoralism he lauds, of "the fair flowers, the fairer forests, the bright valleys and rivers and mountains of the Earth":

> My infant spirit would wake
> To the terror of the lone lake.
> Yet that terror was not fright—
> But a tremulous delight,
> And a feeling undefin'd,
> Springing from a darken'd mind.
> Death was in that poison'd wave
> And in its gulf a fitting grave
> For him who thence could solace bring
> To his dark imagining;
> Whose wild'ring thought could even make
> An Eden of that dim lake.

The strangest argument that the Ideal's absence is poetry's law appears as "The Philosophy of Composition," Poe's supposed account of how he wrote "The Raven." The increasing prominence of the confession in Poe affects his criticism, too, so that this piece reads much like "The Black Cat" or "The Imp of the Perverse." Contradicting the latter, however, Poe here seems to have an "intelligible principle" for casting his lady into the abyss. The opening references to Godwin and Dickens alert us that this is a murder mystery: the narrator of it turns out to be both culprit and detective. The critical voice ratiocinates with increasingly insane lucidity the modus operandi of a poetics whose "most poetical topic" is the death of a beautiful woman. The function of the lady's loss is to evoke "mournful and Never-ending Remembrance," the ultimate in Poe's elevating arabesque states of dissolution. The tension between the essay and the poem lies in the distinction between the lover/student's remembrance and the poet's recollection. Poe explains how willfully the student propounds his questions to the monologocentric bird, ending as intoxicated on "nevermore" as others are by drink, antique volumes, or the contemplation of arabesque tapestries. The raven perches on the bust of Pallas, reminding the student that the attainment of past wisdom, or the return of Lenore, is nevermore. He has a terrible case of Bloom's anxiety, reminded constantly of his belatedness, his loss of the muse, and the probability that he shall never attain (or regain) a philosophical, sexual, or literary Eden. (Not for nothing did Poe contrast his doctrine of mesmeric brevity to the "essential prose" lapses of *Paradise Lost,* as if his own "brief poetical effects" could hypnotize us into forgetting Milton's greatness.) Another parody of the transcendentalist, the student/lover is fanatic in his desire for the immortality of truth and beauty (Lenore).

The poet, however, claims a subtler idea of repetition. "The pleasure" of the poem's refrain, Poe writes, "is deduced solely from the sense of identity—of repetition." Originality is the essay's constant topic, and here Poe sees his way to a literary "originality" that is not that of a single immortal identity: "I determined to produce continuously novel effects, by the variation *of the application* of the *refrain—the refrain* itself remaining, for the most part, unvaried." This principle holds for the combinatorial rhetoric of Poe's borrowings from literary tradition, high and low. The student's arabesque trance brings, not the lady, but a death sentence for transcendentalism; Poe's critical account proceeds to confess the requisite erasure of the center, so that absolute repetition may be eluded. (Poe says he chose "pallas" for its "sonorousness," and we note its homophonic resemblance to "palace" and "phallus," and thus to the haunting of the aristocratic, genealogical transmission of identities.) The eclipse of the light of sense in this case reveals a re-vision of the past, not a vision of the eternally present. Or, more powerfully, we come to see that the eternal and immortal are repetitions, and that the poet, if he is to lay claim to his own identity, must control them. Yet the sorrowful spectacle in Poe's works is usually of protagonists controlled by repetitions, as in the case of the student who is possessed by a compulsion to repeat dead wisdom and dead loves.

Poe's appearance as master of repetition in this narrative reminds us of the other detectives and interpreters in his later work who seem to achieve sublimity in the decoding of mysteries. The skepticism of readers toward the "rational" explanation Poe gives of the composition of "The Raven" is well founded when the dubious achievements of Dupin or Legrand are kept in mind. And reciprocally, we cannot question the ratiocination here without wondering if such genuises are not also perpetrating a hoax. "The Philosophy of Composition," which begins by excluding the role of "accident" or of the unconscious from poetic creation, constitutes the identity of its own originality by the same repression that so evidently divides Poe's protagonists. The mastery of speakers in Poe collapses into the whisperings of their doubles, those discourses of the other which irresistibly come to the "surface" when the text leaps into the abyss of self-reflection. If, as I have argued, all these arabesque states of mind in Poe are structurally coincident with the act of writing, then the terror and fascination is that of the writer who knows (whatever that means) that writing dissolves his own identity, purloins his own character. What does the writer do but put his character(s) in circulation? Don't his inevitable displacements and borrowings, and the unconscious figurations of himself in the work, undo his control, make him yet another letter to be purloined in the reading game?

Dupin, as double of the Minister D——, is both poet and mathematician. He continues the traits of earlier Poe heroes, though the cool intuition of transcendent rationality now replaces the ecstatic state of revelation. The fundamental rule of mathematical calculation in this context is noncontradiction: integers must be identical to themselves. One must not be two or ten, else their systematic combination would prove nonsense. Nor must we inquire too closely into the hypothetical necessity of a zero for the system, lest we be drawn into interminable reflections on the interdependence of being and nothingness. The discrimination of identities, the routing of letters back to their homes or of aberrant crimes to their ordered place, is Dupin's primary activity. In "The Murders in the Rue Morgue," the linguistic puzzle allows Dupin to become an accomplice to the exclusion of forbidden sexual passions from human life and language, as he deduces the nonidentity of the orangutang's voice with any human speech. Though this may be a "correct" solution to the story's surface mystery, it is a very deluded explanation of the other within us that has unspeakable desires. The strength of Dupin's (I can't help hearing "dupe") repression is measurable by the hyperbolic care taken in the solemn incrimination of the orangutang. That this animal could be identified with us is a possibility Dupin never entertains, and is thus the one we are made to fasten on. So obviously *outré* is this poor orangutang that readers who accept it merely replay Dupin's own interpretive blindness. This hint of possible interpretive mastery on *our* part, however, for outsmarting Dupin, won't survive the more complicated exchange of identities in "The Purloined Letter."

Dupin's discourse on method in that tale concerns a schoolboy's victorious strategy in the guessing game of even and odd. The boy guesses his opponent's moves through "an identification of the reasoner's intellect with that of his opponent." The analytical reasoner turns himself into the object of scrutiny by becoming the other: "I fashion the expression of my face . . . in accordance with the expression of his, and then wait to see what thoughts or sentiments arise in my mind or heart, as if to match or correspond with the expression." This purloining of character replays the Romantic idea of sympathetic knowledge. In this game, the analytical player erases himself, takes the place of the other, and hopes to profit by the reflection (as indeed the Minister D—— hands over a check for 50,000 francs). Yet we cannot be so simple as to assume a strict correspondence between surface expression and subjectivity, or to think that a binary calculus of reversals ("If he thinks that I think that he thinks . . ." etc.) will suffice. Poe puns mercilessly on "correspond," having Emerson at least in mind and cautioning against a too easy belief in the transmission of identities. Identification with another may be perilous if human subjectivity is heterogeneous or multiple. Which of the other's selves do we identify with, and with which one of our selves do we do it? Through identification we might take into ourselves the others within the other, and deposit them unknowingly in our own unconscious (as we do all the time when we read). Dupin's method depends upon faith in a mastery of what comes about during the arabesque state of being besides oneself under the influence of some other, and upon a concomitant belief in the proper meaning of characters. The story's complications show up the method's fallacies.

The "origin" of the story, however, as Derrida emphasizes, is in the usurpation of the King's authority and mastery by the Queen's evident adultery. The "phallogocentric" letter demonstrates the wandering of meaning from its "proper" home. In restoring the letter to the Queen, Dupin does not return the letter to its proper place, for it can have none, not even where it is addressed. The power of the letter is in the absence of a univocal meaning, in a vulnerability to interpretation that enables its circulation among purloiners who thus "correspond" with each other. The unrevealed "content" of the letter never concerns Dupin, for he has substituted a semiotic game of placement for the hermeneutic game of meaning. His semiotics of the letter restores the idea of the letter's having a proper place, but it does so only through a systematic structuralist blindness that prevents him from reading its other addresses, or his own displacement within the correspondence. Again, he doubles the Minister D——, who is "blinded" and loses the letter when Dupin's hired agents distract him with a staged disturbance in the street below, firing off a musket into a crowd of women and children. Dupin authors a violent primal scene to recapture the letter, and thus hopelessly entangles himself in representations of transgression, castration, ejaculation, and dissemination. Dupin's dream of control is exquisitely expressed in his victorious pronouncement that "the pretended lunatic was a man in my own pay." This triumphant scene, as Dupin narrates it, will within a page become an ironic commentary on Dupin's own blindness to the implications of the inscription he has left in the purloined letter's double.

Dupin is a superficial reader. His deriding of the Prefect for seeking the letter in depths or secret places expresses his wish to avoid private parts. Dupin keeps himself at a distance, theoretically, from depths and abysses. He falls into one, however, through the reading of letters, because the acts of identification in interpretation require the displacement of our own identities and open up the possibility that the other within may engage in correspondences of an illicit, rather than divine, kind with others elsewhere. The maelstrom here is textual, in that reading is read as an arabesque excitement of the mind that may not result in apocalyptic characters, but in the purloining of ourselves. Poe's own writings offer abundant evidence that the act of writing may precipitate disturbing and unwanted revelations, both within the text and within the mind of the reader.

Dupin himself suffers such a fate. At story's end, some perverse impulse prompts him to leave an incriminating signature within the "fac-simile" that he puts in the place of the re-purloined letter. His desire for recognition stems from an old grudge with the Minister D——, and in this inscription he would seem to have achieved a triumphant announcement of his identity as the master. Simple, but odd. The quote, which takes the place of his proper name, is lifted by Poe from Crébillion's rewrite of the tragedy of the House of Atreus. As Riddel has keenly shown, that ancient revenge plot of adultery, theft, revenge, and cursed genealogy seems one that these Parisians are compelled to repeat. Dupin thus sends a letter to D——, but the "letters" belong to another writer. Dupin changes into a character from an old story, and it is unclear in reflection just who is writing who. Revenge is the parable of repetition par excellence, for its machinery dictates a binary choice of roles (victim or avenger) that reverse with each act, thus reducing the identities of the players to the script's tyranny. Dupin sacrifices his own identity and originality to produce an effect on the Minister

D——, and thereby too becomes an odd letter needing interpretation, and the probable victim of D——'s next move. Dupin wants to strike back for an "evil turn" done him by D—— in Vienna, but we may surmise from Poe's purloining of the Atreus legend that Dupin has been acting all along in unconscious correspondence with a primal, ancient, internalized plot. "Nil sapientiae odiosius acumine nimio."

The primal scene here is represented as that "evil turn" in Vienna, a troping which other critics rightly guess to have a romantic content. If the Minister D—— first purloined a lady from Dupin there, then Dupin's rescue of the Queen would put him back into the position of power or possession regarding the woman that he lost to D—— (the summary easily falls into psychomachia). But unless Dupin (and here's a wish fulfillment) is the author of the "original" purloined letter, then the story ends with Dupin in a position of holding only the "truth" of the letter's endless circulation, or with the sublimated ecstasy of his own apparent victory. If we read that "evil turn" as a symbolic castration of Dupin, then we may understand how giving the phallogocentric letter back to the Queen revenges him. Now the Minister D—— is impotent. The phantom King, however, this story's deepest absence, still remains dispossessed of his power and his property. The Queen meanwhile holds an instrument of power that works only in the absence, blindness, or impotence of the reigning Logos. The truth of letters may not be centered in a transcendental home of meaning, for the power of letters depends on their impropriety and indirection. And of course Poe's own text is itself "The Purloined Letter," subject to all these reflections, and a correspondence course in writing's adultery of identity.

III

In sum, the Romantic or Idealist visionary moment of the soul's knowing union with the world becomes in Poe the nightmare of the self's inhabitation by conflicting scripts. This is not to question the strength of Poe's imaginative lamps, but rather to question the identity or location of authorship. When the text negotiates a rhetorical conflict of repression and expression, who writes? Who authors our nightmares? Poe's work shows a morbid sensitivity to this issue, in its narrators (who scarcely know what they say), in its plots (whose characters seem condemned to repeat old stories), and most literally in his "modernist" deployment of quotes, phrases, ideas, characters, names, and fabulated citations taken (consciously or not) from other writers. These traces form the archive of Poe's rhetoric of borrowing, his cryptic writing or his *écriture*. Commenting on the latter term, Richard Poirier has recently said,

> The performing self is never free of its environment, never a so called "imperial" or unconditioned self. No such thing exists in the history of literature, no self ever has been successfully imperial, because nature (and not just the repressiveness of our selves) dictates that the only materials a "free" self can be constructed from are those by which it is imprisoned.

Poirier goes on to defend Emerson against the charge that he was happily oblivious to the traces of the *écriture* against which self-reliance struggles. Poe often used that reading of Emerson as naive idealist for his straw imperial man. In Emerson, Poe could see the combination of Romantic and German themes united in this pronouncement of Hegel's: "The tendency of all man's endeavors is to understand the world, to appropriate and subdue it to himself; and to this end the positive reality of the world must be as it were crushed and pounded, in other words, idealized." Emerson's self-reliance hoped to put the self back into mastery of its own house. Freud's "call to introspection" was Concord's historical dilemma, as Emerson himself described it: "The young men were born with knives in their brain, a tendency to introversion, self-dissection, anatomizing of motives." The apparent intent of "The American Scholar," "Self-Reliance," and "The Over-Soul" is to purge introversion of historicity, to free self-consciousness from personal or cultural determinations of *écriture*.

Ever since the Pilgrims, the American experiment had been to write a revised script on the new land, to constitute and declare an independent identity to resist and redirect the legacy of the Old World. The central text for interpretation was first the Bible, then the political documents of the Revolution, and then what Emerson called "Nature," a "not-me" including culture as a component. Mingling Kant, Coleridge, and Cotton Mather, Emerson formulates philosophy, poetry, and self as grounded in the reading of this Nature: "A life in harmony with Nature, the love of truth and of virtue, will purge the eyes to understand her text." Emerson tries to imagine the purgation of our consciousness of other in his audacious introduction to *Nature,* which cries out for a liberation from the "dry bones of the past." In the place of the repressed influences of the past, Emerson posits the inspiration of Nature's Over-Soul as the center of the introspective self: "Our being is descending into us from we know not whence. . . . I desire, and look up, and put myself in the attitude of reception, but from some alien energy the visions come." This "Revelation" is "always attended by the emotion of the sublime. For this communication is an influx of the Divine mind into our mind." An "ecstasy," "trance," and "certain tendency to insanity" afflict such visionaries, but the light is the Word, and "Revelation is the disclosure of the soul."

Emerson's "influx of the Divine" appears in Poe as the corpse of the sublime. Where Emerson's self-reliant introspection discovers Eternal Identity, Poe's horrified introverts disclose the anomaly of the Living Dead, the mortality of Beauty and Truth, the puzzle of inscriptions and the collapse of identities into their speculative doubles. Harold Bloom, anxious to make Emerson his precursor prophet of earliness, claims "that a poetic repression brings about the Sublime wildness of freedom." Once more Bloom tries to make repetition a master's game, but he can only do so by ruling out his antagonist from the start. Bloom must "deny the usefulness of the Unconscious, as opposed to repression, as a literary term." With the discourses of the other excluded, the "wildness of freedom" follows as an ineluctable wish fulfillment. Poe's texts insistently put the unconscious in the same structural position (culturally, psychologically, even cosmically) as the Over-Soul, or, more accurately, his writing suggests that the Over-Soul is a strategically adopted persona of the unconscious.

Hegel's method was to make the negations and divisions of the self dialectical. The spirit

> sunders itself to self-realization. But this position of severed life has in its turn to be suppressed, and the spirit has by its own act to win its way to concord again. The final concord then is spiritual; that is, the principal restoration is found in thought, and thought only. The hand that inflicts the wound is also the hand which heals it.

(Emerson would have delighted in the felicity of a translation that made the "final concord" spiritual.) Poe, however, fears the metempsychosis or immortal spirit of written thoughts, their ghostly persistence. In "The Power of Words," two spirits talk of the infinity of influence, taking as their mode the original immortality of the Word:

> It is indeed demonstrable that every such impulse *given the air,* must, *in the end,* impress every individual thing that exists *within the universe;*—and the being of infinite understanding—the being whom we have imagined—might trace the remote undulations of the impulse—trace them upward and onward in their influences upon all particles of all matter—upward and onward for

ever in their modifications of old forms—or, in other words, *in their creation of new*—until he found them reflected—unimpressive *at last*—back from the throne of the Godhead. . . . And while I thus spoke, did there not cross your mind some thought of the *physical power of words?* Is not every word an impulse on the air?

The hopeful turn of influence into the creation of new forms again expresses the quandary of tradition and the individual talent. That is also the theoretical theme of "The Fall of the House of Usher," in which the "final concord" does not restore the mansion of the self, but instead replays the power of other impulses.

The narrator, at the start of his quest to restore the foundations of sanity, experiences a "depression of soul" in his inability to translate the sight of the Usher building into "aught of the sublime." This may be explained by his separation from Usher: "Although, as boys, we have been even intimate associates, yet I really knew little of my friend." (Compare "William Wilson.") The narrator's rationality has heretofore come from the distancing of something with which he was once intimately associated, and whose return will undo him. The House of Usher is itself Poe's most hyperbolic image for the transmission of influences within the structures we inhabit. And if its "excessive antiquity" and arabesque furnishings were not enough, Poe dwells on the repetition compulsion of this "ancient family." Its "direct line of descent," with "very trifling and very temporary variation," prompts the narrator's thoughts to "the perfect keeping of the character of the premises with the accredited character of the people" (note the pun on "premises"), prompting him to "speculating upon the possible influence which the one, in the long lapse of centuries, might have exercised upon the other." Finally, it is the "undeviating transmission, from sire to son, of the patrimony with the name, which had, at length, so identified the two as to merge the original title of the estate in the quaint and equivocal appellation of 'The House of Usher.'" Like the power of words, this heritage forms a strange "sentience" in the "home of his forefathers," "above all in the long undisturbed endurance of this arrangement, and in its reduplication in the still waters of the tarn." This "arrangement" is a perverse celestial music, an "atmosphere" of the "importunate and terrible influence which for centuries had moulded the destinies" of the Usher family.

Hoping to "annihilate" the "sorrowful impression" the building makes upon him (correlative to the unhappy irruption of the other back into his consciousness, also taking the form of Usher's letter to him), the narrator seeks relief in representations: "I reflected, that a mere different arrangement of the particulars of the scene, of the details of the picture" would suffice. Thus he stops at "the precipitous brink of a black and lurid tarn," where glimmer "the remodelled and inverted images" of the house. Here the abyss is again identified with reflection, our impish perversity in sinking into representations, and the remainder of the tale unfolds in the space of this re-cognition.

The narrator begins with the delusion that such reflection can restore him to himself. He too is remodelled and inverted as he enters this abysmal mansion, where he replaces the doctor and the lady Madeline as Usher's physician and twin. Within this frame Poe once more gives us the story (Usher's) of a belated imagination, his soul a ruin, his Ideality the product of a sensual repression culminating in his sister's premature entombment. Yet the involvement of the narrator changes the familiar pattern. Usher and Madeline live in the narrator's rhetorical house of therapeutic writing. His project is to revise the Poe script so as to save the imagination from the return of the repressed. The final, ghastly comic, staging of this effort comes when the narrator tries to soothe Roderick by reading to him! The "antique volume" is the "Mad Trist" by "Sir Launcelot Canning" (a quaint appellation Poe later used as his own pseudonym). The joke is on everyone, for this text is a copy of a nonexistent original, the only "truly" fictitious work in Usher's library. Poe's invented volume parodies our desire to be canny readers, to pierce the mystery of uncanny stories. The narrator hopes to treat Usher with writing: "I indulged a vague hope that the excitement which now agitated the hypochondriac, might find relief (for the history of mental disorder is full of similar anomalies) even in the extremeness of the folly which I should read." A good pre-Freudian doctor, the narrator wants to take Usher's diseased libidinal energy ("excitement") and sublimate it, cathect or attach it to a safe object. What he doesn't see is that reading may be precisely the cause of such "excitement," and that the redirection of libidinal energy will only repeat, albeit in distortion or displacement, the original structure of impulses the narrator hopes to quiet.

The ensuing spectacle of the interdoubling of reality and literature is ʼ ·ed a "Mad Trist" and illustrates Freud's hypothesis that "the uncanny is nothing else than a hidden, familiar thing that has undergone repression and then emerged from it." The narrator reads on blindly, ignoring how the text awakens the unconscious, while Roderick hears mesmerically the echoing of surface and depth. The narrator agrees evidently with those critics who find literature a means of entertainment, or (and it amounts to the same thing) a salvation from being beside themselves by means of a safe transportation to already privileged truths. This literary episode deconstructs the narrator's rationale of reading, exposes with lunatic hilarity his dominant concern with holding the house of his own sanity together.

The story of the "Mad Trist" invites multiple interpretations. Marie Bonaparte finds it an allegory of the Oedipal struggle, with Ethelred slaying the father to gain the mother; this, for her, would be the content of the repressed. Yet Ethelred's entrance by force into the dwelling of the hermit also repeats the motion of Usher's letter to the narrator, as well as that of the narrator's arrival at Usher's mansion. Ethelred is "drunken," in an arabesque state that empowers him to shatter the door, slay the dragon of fire who has replaced the hermit, and gain the protective shield of authority, "breaking up . . . the enchantment which was upon it." Usher (and others) turn the "Trist" into an allegory of Madeline's return, and thus of the return of Usher's own unconscious desires. Usher, however, also seems to accusingly scream "MADMAN" at the *narrator*. The madness of the narrator would be his rationality in reading, his refusal to recognize the other inhabiting the text. Ethelred could be read as the figure of the narrator's quest to break the enchantment of the unconscious that keeps us from truth. Reading would then be an arabesque liberation of formal powers enabling the slaying of the monstrous other. Ethelred's shield would be his phallogocentric emblem, or so antique romance would have it. Madeline's reappearance for her final mad tryst with Roderick is equally unreadable. She is a representation whose "original" identity (as truth, or as the narrator's unconscious, or as Roderick's sensual self) is multiple, a hall of mirrors, and always enchanting. Her return will destroy both Roderick and the narrator, her other double. The failure of the narrator's talking cure reflects upon himself as the identity of the text he reads is haunted by spectral visitations. The stories-within-stories and interpretations-within-interpretations build to an intensity of overdetermination that exceeds the capacity of any single deciphering consciousness or reading strategy.

The narrator "fled aghast" from the scene of all this attraction and repulsion of correspondences. His own writing effort, and the containment of speculation it desired, shatters along with its chief representative. It had seemed to the narrator as if "the superhuman agency" of Roderick's "utterance" had "found the potency of a spell" to open the door for Madeline's enshrouded body. The "potency" of the narrator's own rationalized ejaculations has, in like manner, inadvertently brought forward the figures of the Ushers from within himself. Their collapse into each other's arms is that "fatal embrace" that is Poe's typical negative union. This would seem to purge the narrator cathartically of the conflicts embodied, and so cure himself, but the treatment is not entirely successful. His last reflection occurs looking back at the house. He sees "the full, setting, and blood-red moon" shining through the widening fissure cutting the house in two. This version of the Romantic trope of moonlight for imagination is tinged by the color of blood, and thus pictures a mind colored by thoughts of sex and death. It is these thoughts, archaic and impulsive, nonidentical with the narrative of self-consciousness, that split open the house of himself. The climactic fall of the mansion into its own images serves as the best final commentary on the workings of self-reflection in Poe, and on the effect this can have on the identity of a literary text:

> While I gazed, this fissure rapidly widened—there came a fierce breath of the whirlwind—the entire orb of the satellite burst at once upon my sight—my brain reeled as I saw the mighty walls rushing asunder—there was a long tumultuous shouting sound like the voice of a thousand waters—and the deep and dank tarn at my feet closed sullenly and silently over the fragments of the "*House of Usher*."

Poe sets the "*House of Usher*" apart with quotation marks, in italicized script, as if it were the title of a tale. Riddel has correctly read this scene as a textual deconstruction, the story falling into itself, the proper name in fragments. I would, however, end by recalling that textuality should not be a privileged analytical metaphor. These closing lines, like so much of Poe, won't allow us to extract textuality from sexuality. Inspiration has become daemonized and passionate, "a fierce breath of the whirlwind." The anatomy of the red fissure and "mighty walls rushing asunder" combines a vision of abysmal vaginal horrors with echoes of apocalypse, as if this were a creation catastrophe. The "long tumultuous shouting sound like the voice of a thousand waters" reminds us that the house of generation is both echoic and spermatic: Bloom is right to insist that writing is a family romance, a history of relations. This climax consummates the affair of sex and writing, makes that coupling the final terror, and images its reburial in reflection. The "silence" of the text's "fragments" is not complete, as writing cannot silence the traces left by those shouting voices of the past, for they are also voices of desire.

Desire inspires both lover and writer. The dialectic of Eros and Thanatos some critics find in Poe ought to be replaced by an analytics of eros and *écriture*. One may prematurely bury the corpus of this dilemma, this peculiar intimacy, "sullenly" put it in its place, but the very act of interment leaves its epitaph in script and capital letters. "US" and "HER," tomb of the lovers, house of the poet's relation to the Muse, of Everyman to his Unconscious. The house of writing both participates in and violates the economy of sex. These fragments and fissures picture another castration, a textual/sexual *sparagmos* of the proper that follows from the primal scene of Roderick and Madeline's "Mad Trist." Yet the dissemination of these "thousand waters" generates the recapitation of the *"House of Usher."* Tomb, phallus, text, the *"House of Usher"* rises up at the end in writing, a typographic inverse double of the house and story now disappearing into the tarn. It is, I will suggest, the undecidable significance of this union of sex and writing that makes Poe's work finally "unreadable." The structures of these two discourses embrace without a unifying authority, become rivals for the letter, and draw us as readers into an interminable analysis of textual intercourse.

Phantasms of Death in Poe's Fiction

J. Gerald Kennedy

The tales of Edgar Allan Poe display an elaborate repertoire of supernatural motifs, so well adapted to the evocation of horror that one might suppose the *frisson* to be their exclusive object. Otherwise discerning readers have thus fixed upon such phantasmagoria as evidence of Poe's "pre-adolescent mentality"—to recall the judgment of T. S. Eliot—and concluded that his otherworldly tales amount to little more than gimcrackery. Even those with a scholarly regard for Poe's achievement sometimes assume (as the author invited us to) that mystical elements in the fiction serve mainly to secure the necessary "single effect." Collectively examined, however, his tales reveal the complex function of the supernatural, which typically introduces the predicament that his protagonists must overcome, escape, explain away, or surrender to. The intrusion of the uncanny generates "cosmic panic" (in Lovecraft's phrase) and poses the troubling paradox at the center of Poe's dark vision. Although the preternatural arrives in various shapes—as a demon-horse, a phantom ship, or a reanimated corpse—it commonly dramatizes the interpenetration of life and death, the mingling of metaphysical opposites. A passing glance at the recurrent themes of vampirism, metempsychosis, spiritualism, and spectral manifestation indicates Poe's fixation with the fate of the body and the destiny of the soul. In effect, such motifs carry a significance independent of the narrative scheme in which they emerge; they constitute an esoteric ideography and inscribe a parallel

From *The Haunted Dusk: American Supernatural Fiction, 1820–1920*, edited by Howard Kerr, John W. Crowley, and Charles L. Crow. © 1983 by the University of Georgia Press.

text concerned exclusively with final questions. Through a decoding of this imagery, I want to clarify the four conceptual models which dominated Poe's representation of our mortal condition.

II

Under the ostensible influence of Walpole, Radcliffe, Brockden Brown, Coleridge, Irving, and the German Romantics Tieck and Hoffmann, Poe assimilated the conventions of Gothic Horror. His gravitation toward that mode was probably inevitable, for its narrative configuration seems to have embodied his fundamental perception of the human condition. In his preface to *Tales of the Grotesque and Arabesque* (1840), he described the "terror . . . of the soul" as his essential "thesis." The supernatural paraphernalia of the Gothic, particularly phantasms of death and destruction, afforded a means of articulating this primal fear. In a broad sense, Poe's "terror of the soul" bears traces of the historical and intellectual crisis that produced the Gothic novel; indeed, we cannot make sense of his preoccupation with madness, violence, perverseness, disease, death, and decomposition without recognizing the cultural drama inherent in what David Punter has called the "literature of terror." It is a commonplace notion that the Gothic emerged from the rupture in Western thought between rationalism and Romanticism that occurred in the latter half of the eighteenth century. This formulation, however crude, contains an important truth: Gothic fiction enacts the radical uncertainty of an epoch of revolution in which nearly all forms of authority—neoclassicism, Right Reason, religious orthodoxy, and aristocracy—came to be seen as constricting systems. Ghosts and crumbling castles, wicked lords and diabolical monks served as fictive emblems of a collapsing order. Alone in a landscape of nightmare, the Gothic hero experienced the dark side of Romantic freedom: existential disorientation, wrought by the loss of defining structures. The Gothic paradigm dramatized for the first time the quintessential modern predicament—the plight of an alienated being whose rational skepticism had vitiated his capacity for belief, while paralyzing dread had betrayed the insufficiency of science and logic. It was the peculiar achievement of the Gothic (and, one imagines, the basis of its appeal) to express in playful, imaginative terms the latent fears of Western culture in an urban, industrial, post-rational, and post-Christian era. If this species of fiction presented a search for answers, an elucidation of mysteries, its real force lay, as Punter observes, in the evocation of doubt, in its capacity for "removing the illusory halo of certainty from the so-called 'natural' world."

Through its own illogic, Gothic supernaturalism exposed the limits of reason as an explanatory model. The proliferation of occult themes in eigh-teenth-century literature amounted, in the view of Patricia Meyer Spacks, to a recognition that "the mind of man is naturally subject to secret terrors and apprehensions" and that supernatural motifs possess a "real and uni-versal" validity. Writers of Gothic Fiction, even those like Ann Radcliffe who were committed to an ultimately rational vision, felt the need to widen the range of narrative possibility and draw upon the imagery of dreams. But the insurgence of literary supernaturalism expressed more than a re-sistance to Augustan aesthetic constraints; it also manifested a curious re-sponse to the rationalizing of religious thought in the eighteenth century. In effect, writers of Gothic novels salvaged elements of popular belief—devils, curses, and spiritual visitations—that had been jettisoned by Chris-tian humanist thought. And their use of supernatural imagery appears to have one other major implication: as a response to death in the face of religious skepticism. Glen St. John Barclay has argued that "any story which in any sense refers to the intervention of the supernatural in human affairs necessarily affirms that the supernatural exists. It holds out the reality of alternative modes or realms of existence beyond the physical limitations of our material life. In doing so, it responds directly to what is certainly man's most abiding concern, the prospect of his own personal annihilation and oblivion in death." One must question the inference that any literary rep-resentation of the supernatural affirms its existence in the experiential world—a blatant confusion of art and life—but Barclay's perception of the uncanny in fiction as a response to the fear of "personal annihilation" seems astute. When we consider that the Gothic movement derived much of its impetus from the graveyard school of poetry, we perceive that in the midst of other revolutions in taste, belief, and thought in the eighteenth century, a wholly new and powerful consciousness of death had begun to emerge. In place of the calm acceptance of mortality we might expect in the verse of a clergyman-poet, we find in Young's *Night Thoughts on Death* and Blair's *The Grave* a deepening anxiety about extinction. Such poetry excited cu-riosity about death and decomposition; it introduced dreams and fantasies about dying; and it conferred upon the tomb and the cemetery a peculiar new importance. The abode of death became associated with preternatural phenomena, as instanced by Blair's depiction of a weird procession:

> Roused from their slumbers,
> In grim array the grisly spectres rise,
> Grin horrible, and obstinately sullen
> Pass and repass, hushed as the foot of night.
>
> (ll. 39–42)

Such images proliferated in the mid-eighteenth century as a funereal sensibility infused popular literature; death was no longer simply an event or moment in writing but its very object.

The association of supernaturalism and mortality acquires broader significance in light of the monumental study of Philippe Ariès, *The Hour of Our Death.* Through research into the burial practices, wills, and memorial sculpture of France (and Western culture generally) since the Middle Ages, Ariès demonstrates that, far from being a universal and static phenomenon, our conception of mortality has undergone vast changes, from the serene, public leave-taking of the medieval "tame death" to the lonely despair of our contemporary "invisible death"—the institutional concealment of the final hour. Perhaps the most striking of Ariès's general conclusions is the observation that before the end of the seventeenth century, "human beings as we are able to perceive them in the pages of history [had] never really known the fear of death." Initially this seems a baseless proposition, for the phrase "fear of death" involves an apparent conflation of several distinct responses—to the idea of death, its imminence, its bodily effects, and its psychic consequences. As a historical judgment, this also seems doubtful; we know, for example, that the deadly plagues of the late Middle Ages inspired terror throughout Europe. But we must bear in mind that the medieval fear of an immediate threat and its spiritual corollary fear of eternal judgment are both quite different from the modern dread of mortality, the crux of the general claim. Ariès associates the onset of contemporary death-anxiety with three broad developments: the secularization of death and the erosion of belief in an afterlife; the growth of self-consciousness and individualism, which diminished the communal aspect of death and made it a private, personal experience; and the advent of science and modern medicine, which converted the corpse into an object of study and death into a physiological process. As indices of these changes, we see in the eighteenth century the appearance of public cemeteries and the abandonment of services once provided by the church; the practice of erecting funerary monuments to commemorate the existence of the common folk; the exhuming of bodies for experimental purposes; and, as noted earlier, the appearance of literary and artistic productions concerned with mortality and grief.

One result of scientific attention to the physiology of death was a mounting curiosity about the connection between the body and the soul. The medieval idea of the *homo toto*, the whole and indissoluble man, was supplanted during the Enlightenment by the concept of a self that divided at death. But what part did the soul play in the agony of dying, and where did it go at the moment of extinction? Ariès notes that "this question, which is at the heart of the medical interest in death, is also one of the central preoccupations of the age." Investigations of cadavers exerted a "profound impact on the imagination of the time," feeding speculation about residual sentience in the corpse and about the prospect of galvanic reanimation. Such research demanded fresh anatomical specimens and thus gave rise to the atrocity of grave-robbing. This clandestine industry swiftly generated a folklore of violated tombs and reviving corpses; it must have contributed to the appearance, about 1740, of a terror hitherto unexpressed in Western culture—the fear of premature burial.

III

This upheaval in attitudes touches almost every facet of cultural experience. With respect to Gothic fiction, the ubiquity of corpses (often bleeding preternaturally) reminds us, as Freud would much later, that the ultimate source of all terror is death itself. In effect, the haunted castle, the subterranean passageway, the secret vault, and the sealed room—all the conventional scenes of Gothic mystery—evoke anxiety because they pose the implicit threat of fatal enclosure. In an age that witnessed what Ariès calls "the first manifestation of the great modern fear of death," we discover a literary form given over to the recurrent staging of ultimate vulnerability. But the Gothic did not remain a static form; when we come upon its recognizable contours in the fiction of Poe, we also encounter new resonances and motifs indicative of changes in the cultural consciousness of death.

Perhaps in reaction to the eighteenth century's prolonged contemplation of the unshrouded corpse and the gaping grave, the dark imaginings once poetically associated with death had shaded into a bland sentimentality about time and transience, about loss and separation. By the early nineteenth century, as Ariès points out, the sense of mortality as "pure negativity" accompanied a fascination with the idea of a spiritual reunion beyond the grave. The ghastly image of death created by the procurement and dissection of cadavers yielded to an extravagant, romanticized vision of "the beautiful death"—a tender, well-planned departure, in which the prospect of an otherworldly rendezvous loomed large. Religious sentiment enjoyed a superficial resurgence in consolation literature, as the hour of death became a fetishized event. Ann Douglas has called attention to the necrolatry inherent in these works: "Such writings inflated the importance of dying and the dead by every possible means; they sponsored elaborate methods of burial and commemoration, communication with the next world, and microscopic viewings of a sentimentalized afterlife." The poetry of Felicia Hemans and her American admirer, Lydia Huntley Sigourney, epitomized the movement in popular culture toward an ethereal image of mortality, purged of gross physical detail. Ariès summarizes the prevailing attitude: "Since death is not the end of the loved one, however bitter the grief of the survivor, death is neither ugly nor fearful. On the contrary, death is beautiful, as the dead body is beautiful. Presence at the deathbed in the nineteenth century is more than a customary participation in a social ritual; it is an opportunity to witness a spectacle that is both comforting and exalting." But this new perception involves aesthetic contrivance: "This death [was] no longer death, it [was] an illusion of art." Indeed, the preoccupation with mortality so evident in magazines, annuals, and contemporary engravings betrays massive cultural self-deception: "In life as well as in art and literature, death [was] concealing itself under the mask of beauty."

What these shifts in sensibility reveal most clearly is the essential instability of Western ideas about mortality since roughly 1700. The reassuring model of "familiar and tame" death, prevalent until the late seventeenth century, vanished with the rise of the modern, industrialized, secular city. In its place emerged a multiplicity of conflicting attitudes and assumptions, producing radical confusion about the nature and meaning of death. The Christian message of resurrection continued to be heard, but clergymen as frequently extolled the beauty of dying, outlined the spiritual benefits of grief, or described the amenities of a domesticated heaven. Proponents of spiritualism grew numerous and by the mid-nineteenth century had established an organized movement. Those still influenced by a deistic or pantheistic saw death as Bryant had painted it in "Thanatopis": a beatific return to the bosom of nature, that "mighty sepulchre" of humanity. Attitudes originating in eighteenth-century graveyard verse continued to obtrude upon the popular consciousness; as I have shown in another essay, the fear of premature burial sustained a flourishing fictional subgenre in contemporary periodicals. Medical experiments upon corpses still excited a horrified fascination, as the popularity of Mary Shelley's *Frankenstein* (1819) suggests. The rise of scientific positivism prompted widespread doubts about the existence of an immaterial soul, to the chagrin of ministers and spiritualists alike.

But amid the welter of contending viewpoints, David Stannard has discerned the "overriding national treatment of death" between the Revolution and the Civil War: "In large measure, if not entirely in response to the growing individual anonymity brought on by changes in their social world, Americans sought a return to their lost sense of community in the graveyard and the heavenly world of the dead; in the process, paradoxically, they effectively banished the reality of death from their lives by a spiritualistic and sentimentalized embracing of it." That is, the death fetish of the early nineteenth century grew from a need to reestablish bonds of commitment in an increasingly impersonal, urban society. But in order for death to become the great Meeting Place, it had to be disinfected and prettified. The effort to invest death with sentimentalized beauty drew the support of many leading writers; Washington Irving's tales "The Pride of the Village" and "The Broken Heart" (in *The Sketch-Book*) epitomize the tearful fare that flooded the publishing scene, promoting the Beautiful Death. This was the very society that, in Mark Twain's *Huckleberry Finn*, produced the lachrymose Emmeline Grangerford: "She warn't particular, she could write about anything you choose to give her to write about, just so it was sadful. Every time a man died, or a woman died, or a child died, she would be on hand with her 'tribute' before he was cold." With respect to popular gift book poetry, there is less exaggeration in Twain's caricature than one would suppose.

IV

Such was the literary and cultural environment in which Poe endeavored to sustain himself as a writer in the early 1830s. That he found the funereal sentimentality of the day a valid rhetorical mode may be surmised from his appreciative regard for Mrs. Sigourney, Letitia E. Landon, Mrs. E. Clementine Stedman, and other purveyors of maudlin stuff. In 1842 he did score the "namby-pamby character" of *Graham's Magazine* in a moment of pique, but there is no evidence that he found the cultural preoccupation with mortality unhealthy, inappropriate, or laughable. By temperament and mournful personal experience, Poe was drawn into the contemporary cult of death. But if he respected the muse of sentiment, he avoided in his tales the conventional sad-but-joyful departure, and he clearly saw through the "mask of beauty" that concealed the grim features of human dissolution. In his "Marginalia" series Poe observed trenchantly, "Who ever *really* saw anything but horror in the smile of the dead? We so earnestly *desire* to fancy it 'sweet'—that is the source of the mistake; if, indeed, there ever was a mistake in the question." Unlike his contemporaries, he refused to soften or idealize mortality and kept the essential "horror" in view; but he also moved beyond the Gothic formula to explore divergent conceptions of death. Through the symbolic notation provided by supernatural motifs, we can identify the features of four principal paradigms: annihilation, compulsion, separation, and transformation.

Annihilation. In his illuminating study *The Denial of Death,* Ernest Becker builds his argument upon a fundamental insight: "This is the meaning of the Garden of Eden myth and the rediscovery of modern psychology: that death is man's peculiar and greatest anxiety." This comment goes far in explaining the stunning contemporaneity of Poe's fiction and poetry. Becker's analysis demonstrates that we experience death as a "complex symbol" that changes as human beings pass through successive stages of consciousness. But the primal, embedded meaning of death, which all of our "immortality projects" seek to overcome, is that of terrifying annihilation. Initially encountered in childhood through the permanent disappearance of loved ones, this terror develops finally into a concept of personal extinction, a recognition of one's creaturely condition—that one is trapped within a body that "aches and bleeds and will decay and die." This elemental anxiety informs much of Poe's fiction; it manifests itself in the wild, deathbed protest of Ligeia: "O God! O Divine Father!—shall these things be undeviatingly so?—shall this Conqueror be not once conquered?" The Conqueror Worm, its "vermin fangs / In human gore imbued," provides a graphic reminder of our bodily fate. An acute interest in the physiology and physical imagery of death in fact typifies Poe's annihilation model. Visible signs of disease, impending death, or dissolution assume as reminders of the ultimate naturalistic process. Poe also draws attention to traditional emblems of death—the skull, the skeleton, the "grim reaper," the moldering corpse—to intensify the anxiety of his protagonists (cf. "The Pit and the Pendulum"). As a metaphorical reminder that one is, to borrow the later phrase of Yeats, "fastened to a dying animal," the annihilation paradigm in Poe frequently involves physical entrapment aboard a ship, inside a house, within a vortex, behind a wall, or (most revealingly) in the tomb itself.

Elements of this model can be found in most of Poe's tales, but its purest expression occurs in "Shadow—A Parable" and in the more impressive sequel, "The Masque of the Red Death." These works have in common an atmosphere of brooding anticipation. Both represent the deliberate immurement of a group fearful of pestilence, and both depict the physical intrusion of death. Each tale implicitly suggests that our most ingenious strategies cannot protect us from this fate, nor can we entirely repress the dread to which that awareness gives rise. Significantly, I think, neither story raises the prospect of a happy reunion in another world. "Shadow" closes with the perception by the "company of seven" of a multitude of spirit voices, "the well remembered and familiar accents of many thousand departed friends," but far from providing reassurance, these voices cause the assemblage to start from their seats "in horror, and stand trembling, and shuddering, and aghast." The annihilation model presents a stark encounter with the death-anxiety from which our "neurotic shield" of repression ordinarily protects us.

As the headnote to "Shadow" makes clear, the title figure is the shadow of death, whose presence imposes a palpable depression: "There were things around us and about which I can render no distinct account—things material and spiritual—heaviness in the atmosphere—a sense of suffocation—anxiety—and, above all, that terrible sense of existence which the nervous experience when the senses are keenly living and awake, and meanwhile the powers of thought lie dormant. A dead weight hung upon us . . . ; and all things were depressed, and borne down thereby." Death weighs upon the group because it is thrice present: first in the pallid countenances of the men themselves as reflected on the ebony table; then in the corpse of "young Zoilus," whose unclosed eyes reveal a "bitterness" (even though the body is "enshrouded"); finally in the "dark and undefined shadow" that issues from the sable draperies and fixes itself upon the door. Here, the supernatural impinges upon the natural world to signify an important concept. The "vague, and formless, and indefinite" shadow, a manifestation "neither of man, nor of God, nor of any familiar thing," projects a view of death as terrifying absence and absolute difference. Its horror derives from its complete unintelligibility. Poe's conception of the shadow also relates mortality to the idea of evil, for the inscription sets up an inherent contrast between the Psalmist, who will "fear no evil" in the valley of the shadow of death, and the narrator Oinos, who suffers "the boding and the memory of evil" within the sealed room. According to Ariès, death lost much of its sacral quality in the eighteenth century when men ceased to believe in hell and "the connection between death and sin or spiritual punishment." No longer a moment of religious significance, the hour of reckoning, death itself became evil, a thing to be avoided. (We begin to see the importance of this association for Poe when we note the elements of the human tragedy specified in the "The Conqueror Worm": Madness, Sin, and Horror.)

A slightly different emphasis develops in "The Masque of the Red Death," where the situation adumbrated in "Shadow" acquires complexity and dramatic effect. There is no need here to review extant interpretations of the tale's color symbolism, nor should we be detained by the "ebony clock," with its too-obvious linking of time and death. What demands closer scrutiny is Poe's characterization of the dreadful intruder and the implications of that portrayal. Cutting through a tangle of critical conjecture, Joseph Patrick Roppolo has called the work "a parable of the inevitability and universality of death." Death cannot be barred from the palace, he argues, because it is in the blood, part and parcel of our humanity, not an external invader. Hence, according to Roppolo, the spectral figure is not a representation of mortality (which is already present) but a figment of the imagination: man's "self-aroused and self-developed fear of his own mistaken concept of death."

This approach has a certain validity—death is indeed in our blood, coded in our genes—and it leads to the interesting hypothesis that Prospero succumbs to his own terror, to the "mistaken" idea that death is a tangible enemy. But it also collapses the supernaturalism of the story and reduces the intriguing figure to a simple misconception, thus distorting the allegorical signification. The notion of the specter as self-delusion loses credibility when we realize that all of the revellers observe "the presence of a masked figure." Either everyone deludes himself in precisely the same way, or else there *is* a figure. Poe's careful description of the "spectral image," as he is seen by "the whole crowd," supports the latter view.

> The figure was tall and gaunt, and shrouded from head to foot in the habiliments of the grave. The mask which concealed the visage was made so nearly to resemble the countenance of a stiffened corpse that the closest scrutiny must have had difficulty in detecting the cheat. And yet all this might have been endured, if not approved, by the mad revelers around. But the mummer had gone so far as to assume the type of the Red Death. His vesture was dabbled in *blood*—and his broad brow, with all the features of the face, was besprinkled with the scarlet horror.

In choosing to symbolize the unmentionable, the "mummer" has violated a taboo and brought death into the open. But why does Poe insist upon the particularity of the Red Death imagery? In the opening paragraph he describes the plague as extraordinarily fatal and hideous: "there were sharp pains, and sudden dizziness, and then profuse bleeding at the pores, with dissolution." Even more terrible, "the whole seizure, progress and termination of the disease, were the incidents of half an hour." That is, the Red Death produces grotesque disfiguration and almost instantaneous decomposition (the horror of M. Valdemar). The putrefaction of the grave becomes a public spectacle as the plague transforms a vibrant individual into a loathsome object. Belief in the uniqueness of personality and the immortality of the soul crumbles at the sight of human carrion. The Red

Death evokes dread because it exposes our creatureliness and raises the question at the core of naturalistic thought: are we finally nothing more than the biological organization of our own perishable flesh?

Such appears to be Poe's conclusion, at least in this parable of annihilation, for when the masqueraders fall upon the stranger, they discover an emptiness behind the corpselike mask.

> Then, summoning the wild courage of despair, a throng of revellers at once threw themselves into the black apartment, and, seizing the mummer, whose tall figure stood erect and motionless within the shadow of the ebony clock, gasped in unutterable horror at finding the grave cerements and corpselike mask which they handled with so violent a rudeness, untenanted by any tangible form.

This discovery reenacts the nineteenth-century perception of death as "pure negativity," a nullity resulting from the "separation of the body and the soul" (Ariès). Poe's portrayal of pure absence signifies "the presence of the Red Death"; the revellers fall, the clock stops, and "the flames of the tripods" expire. Pestilence holds dominion with "Darkness and Decay" over the realm of human experience. The silence of the mummer reigns, and for Poe, silence nearly always implies both the death of the body and the extinction of the soul. In "Sonnet—Silence," written three years before "The Masque of the Red Death," Poe distinguished between "the corporate Silence," which has "no power of evil . . . in himself," and "his shadow," the nameless and (by implication) evil silence that is the death of the spirit. The wordless figure who comes "like a thief in the night," bringing silence to Prospero's domain, presents but a semblance of physical death; he is actually the more dreadful incorporeal silence that affirms the annihilation of the soul.

Compulsion. In "The Imp of the Perverse," Poe accounts for the irrational urge to cast one's self from a precipice, to plunge into an abyss: "And this fall—this rushing annihilation—for the very reason that it involves that one most ghastly and loathsome of all the most ghastly and loathsome images of death and suffering which have ever presented themselves to our imagination—for this very cause do we now the most vividly desire it." This passage at once epitomizes the compulsion paradigm and suggests its relationship to the model already discussed. Death-as-compulsion draws upon the terror of annihilation but finds within it an irrational pleasure, "the delight of its horror." The disgusting character of death, which generates anxiety and aversion in the previous form, now becomes an object of fascination and longing. In *The Narrative of Arthur Gordon Pym* and "A Descent into the Maelström," Poe associated the "perverse" with the image of the abyss, a self-evident symbol of engulfing mortality, and thus indicated its patently suicidal nature. In other works dramatizing the perverse—"The Tell-Tale Heart," "The Black Cat," and "The Cask of Amontillado"—the literal abyss becomes an implied figure disclosed by temptation: the "unfathomable longing of the soul *to vex itself*—to offer violence to its own nature" through displaced self-destructiveness. In each of these tales, an act of murder leads to obsessive revelation; "The Imp of the Perverse" makes explicit the suicidal impulse of the confession: "They say that I spoke with a distinct enunciation, but with marked emphasis and passionate hurry, as if in dread of interruption before concluding the brief but pregnant sentences that consigned me to the hangman and to hell."

Although the death-wish theory of Freud has been largely discredited, the longing for an end to life has (as Eliot's headnote to *The Waste Land* suggests) a persistent tradition of its own. Since the rise of Romanticism, the will to die has become increasingly conspicuous in Western culture. Roughly concurrent with the rise of the Gothic novel and the valorization of "sensibility," Goethe's *Sorrows of Young Werther* (1774) "swept over eighteenth-century Europe like a contagious disease," initiating a vogue for suicide—or, more precisely, unleashing an impulse that had long been held in check by reason, faith, and social convention. Four years before *Werther*, the self-induced death of Thomas Chatterton had had only a limited impact, but in the wake of Goethe's novel and its literary progeny, Chatterton's death became an important symbol: he was, for the Romantics, "the first example of death by alienation." The outbreak of suicide in life and literature in the late eighteenth century expresses far more than a passing fashion; it seems to manifest an intriguing response to the modern dread of death. At first glance, this seems an illogical supposition: how does the wish for death follow from the fear of mortality? We know know that in some cases thanatophobia paradoxically drives the individual toward death as a means of release from the burden of death-anxiety. We understand too that the act on some basic level involves a rejection of the fated biological creature; the mind or self directs violence against the body to eradicate the pain and despair inevitably experienced in the viscera. Hence the Romantic vogue for suicide, which finds expression in Poe, reflects yet another aspect of the quintessential modern affliction that Kierkegaard called the "sickness unto death."

Two of Poe's early tales, "Metzengerstein" and "MS. Found in a Bottle," use supernatural motifs to illuminate the inner world of suicidal compulsion. In "Metzengerstein" a "mysterious steed" seems to embody the soul of the hated Count Berlifitzing, and by carrying the Baron Metzengerstein to his death, it enforces a curse and completes the revenge pattern. But attention to detail indicates that the horse actually embodies the fiendish malignancy of the baron himself, whose "perverse attachment" to the animal stems from an intrinsic likeness: "the young Metzengerstein seemed riveted to the saddle of that colossal horse, whose intractable audacities so well accorded with his own spirit." The beast inspires an instinctive dread: Metzengerstein "never vaulted into the saddle, without an unaccountable and almost imperceptible shudder"; he never names the horse and never places his hand "upon the body of the beast." His fear originates from his first perception of the horse as a tapestried image. Significantly, Poe writes that the baron feels an "overwhelming anxiety" that falls "like a pall upon his senses." The nature of his terror becomes explicit when a preternatural change in the horse's features discloses its symbolic function: "The eyes, before invisible, now wore an energetic and human expression, while they gleamed with a fiery and unusual red; and the distended lips of the apparently enraged horse left in full view his sepulchral and disgusting teeth." Once again, Poe associates evil (the fiery, hellish eyes) with death (the sepulchral teeth) in contriving an image of Metzengerstein's inescapable doom. But here is the essence of the compulsion model: far from banishing the symbol of his future destruction, Metzengerstein compulsively surrenders himself to the creature (and the horror he inspires), finally allowing the horse to carry him into the all-consuming flames.

"MS. Found in a Bottle" adds a significant dimension to this conception of death by suggesting that the narrator seeks more than his own perverse annihilation: he longs to enter the abyss, the vortex, to glimpse the *mysterium tremendum* it contains. In the tale's most frequently cited passage, Poe juxtaposes the terror of extinction and the yearning to pierce the veil of mortality: "To conceive the horror of my sensations is, I presume, utterly impossible; yet a curiosity to penetrate the mysteries of these awful regions, predominates even over my despair, and will reconcile me to the most hideous aspect of death. It is evident that we are hurrying onwards to some exciting knowledge—some never-to-be-imparted secret, whose attainment is destruction." The story's dense supernaturalism virtually obliges one to understand "these awful regions" as a reference to death, for the voyage itself is a parable of the passage toward it. Shortly after its departure from Java, the freighter on which the narrator sails is becalmed in a manner reminiscent of the ship in Coleridge's *Ancient Mariner*. The stillness, a foretoken of death's fixity, expresses itself in two signs: "The flame of a candle burned on the poop without the least perceptible motion, and a long hair, held between the finger and thumb, hung without the possibility of detecting a vibration." Readers of Poe's day would have recognized in these details two familiar methods of verifying death in cases of suspended animation. The analogy becomes more apparent when the sun is suddenly "extinguished by some unaccountable power," plunging the ship into the "pitchy darkness" of "eternal night" and the narrator into a condition of anxiety and "utter hopelessness." Poe's introduction of the phantom ship—appropriately colored a "deep dingy black"—contributes images of aging to the increasingly complex death symbolism; the spectral sailors personify decay, the ineluctable failure of the flesh: "Their knees trembled with infirmity; their shoulders were bent double with decrepitude; their shrivelled skins rattled in the wind; their voices were low, tremulous, and broken; their eyes glistened with the rheum of years; and their gray hairs streamed terribly in the tempest." Yet these wasted figures, phantasms of the narrator's own never-to-be-reached senescence, inspire a "sentiment ineffable," for they approach the fatal vortex with "more of the eagerness of hope than of the apathy of despair." Their immense age and acceptance of death fill the narrator with a sense of novelty and expectation, and so despite irrepressible sensations of horror, he awaits a potential revelation. In this sense the tale of compulsion looks forward to two other models—separation and transformation—in which death is both an end and a beginning.

Separation. In an age that cultivated the idea of the "the Beautiful Death," the last hour became a matter of extravagant preparation. Those stricken with a lingering illness (tuberculosis was the fashionable malady) made the most of their invalidism by composing letters, poems, diaries, and meditational works, filled with reflections upon earthly life and hopes for the hereafter. Belief in a spiritual rendezvous introduced an element of joyous expectancy to the deathbed scene, Ariès notes, but it also caused death itself to be regarded as "an intolerable separation." The parting became a ritualistic event; the offering of flowers—to beautify the image of death—entered into common usage, as did the creation of commemorative jewelry, needlework, and painting. Ariès characterizes this pattern of funereal idolatry as "the death of the Other" because in an important sense, death became an object of scrutiny and the dying person a kind of aesthetic component, an element in the tableau of "the Beautiful Death." This transformation could only have occurred through a suppression of the physiology of decay and the dissociation of mortality from a concept of hell. Ariès remarks, "No sense of guilt, no fear of the beyond remained to counteract the fascination of death, transformed into the highest beauty."

Without the threat of damnation, the notion of heaven also changed, becoming "the scene of the reunion of those whom death has separated but
who have never accepted this separation."

Poe's valorization of "the death of a beautiful woman" as "the most
poetical topic in the world" thus exploited a common theme in nineteenth-
century culture. In poem after poem, his persona experiences the death of
a woman as a radical separation from the beloved Other, an estrangement
inducing guilt, grief, madness, and lonely visits to the tomb of the deceased.
The sequence of stories from "Berenice" through "The Oval Portrait" uses
the same poetic premise but with some intriguing modifications: in fiction,
the woman's death excites horror, even perverse impatience in the narrator,
who observes disgusting physical changes, in place of the beatific reunion
of spirits envisioned in consolation literature, Poe dramatized an implicit
antagonism, sometimes culminating in a frenzied, mad encounter with the
buried woman. The notable exception to this scheme is "Eleonora," a tale
that embodies fairly conventional ideas of death and spiritual communion.
More representative of Poe's separation paradigm, however, are "Morella"
and "Ligeia," works that depict death not as absolute annihilation but as
an ambiguous, temporary parting. In a monstrous parody of the death of
the Other, Poe represents the return of the beloved not in spiritual terms
but as a ghastly reincarnation tinged with vampirism. Through such supernaturalism, he implies that death is neither an extinction of the self nor
admission to a heavenly social club. Rather, it is a condition of spiritual
confinement and unrest, a dream world where one acts out the desires and
hostilities of an earlier existence.

"Morella" dramatizes a metaphysical question that troubled Poe's
generaton: his narrator ponder the fate of individual essence—the "principium individuationis, the notion of that identity which at death is or is not lost
forever." The tale seems to confirm the survival of personal entity when
the dying wife ostensibly returns in the person of the daughter whom she
has delivered upon her deathbed; the empty tomb, discovered at the story's
end, implies the transmigration of the mother's soul. But the story also
raises a doubt about the idea of an enduring, transferable identity, for death
of the "second Morella" apparently brings to a close the cycle of resurrection. Less ambiguously, the narrative demonstrates Poe's characteristic at-
traction-repulsion pattern: the narrator's "singular affection" for Morella
and the abandon with which he enters into a mystical apprenticeship give
way at length to "horror" and "alienation." As in "Berenice," the onset
of physical decline obsesses the narrator: "In time, the crimson spot settled
steadily upon the cheek, and the blue veins upon the pale forehead became

prominent; and one instant, my nature melted into pity, but, in the next, I met the glance of her meaning eyes, and then my soul sickened and became giddy with the giddiness of one who gazes downward into some dreary and unfathomable abyss." This is a fascinating passage: the narrator observes the signs of his wife's impending death and feels himself caught helplessly in a mechanism of self-destruction (the compulsion model). Her extinction somehow entails his own.

Here Poe touches upon the human tendency to feel jeopardized by the vulnerability or aging of one's partner. Ernest Becker notes that "if a woman loses her beauty, or shows that she doesn't have the strength and dependability that we once thought she did," men may experience the ultimate threat: "The shadow of imperfection falls over our lives, and with it—death and the defeat of cosmic heroism. 'She lessens' = 'I die.'" The narrator's revulsion should be understood not as a response to Morella herself but to her mortality; we can trace his disgust back to her "cold hand," to the voice whose melody is "tainted with terror," to the "melancholy eyes"—all signs of the fate she anticipates and symbolizes. His abhorrence of the process of dissolution and his eagerness for the moment of release foreshadow the twentieth-century concept of unspeakable, invisible death—the hidden shame we encounter, unforgettably, in Tolstoy's "The Death of Ivan Ilych."

In effect, "Morella" presents a grotesque inversion of the sweet parting idealized as "the Beautiful Death." The dread evoked by the death of the Other seems central to this model: in "Berenice" the narrator's "insufferable anxiety" leads to the unconscious defilement of his cousin's body; in "The Fall of the House of Usher" Roderick's terror prevents him from voicing his suspicion that Madeline has been interred prematurely; in "The Oval Portrait" the painter grows "tremulous and very pallid, and aghast" as he perceives the fate of his wife. Fear and loathing enter the scheme of "Ligeia" in a different way. After witnessing his wife's fierce struggle to overcome death through a sheer act of will, the narrator remarries and projects his repressed disgust upon Rowena. The image of his second wife's "pallid and rigid figure upon the bed" brings to mind Ligeia's death and "the whole of that unutterable woe with which [he] had regarded *her* thus enshrouded." During the "hideous drama of revivification," Rowena's morbid relapses produce two associated effects: the narrator's shudder of horror at "the ghastly expression of death" and his "waking vision of Ligeia." The mingling of past and present pushes the narrator to the brink of madness: the woman before him is both living and dead, Lady Rowena and Ligeia, an impossible fusion of irreconcilable opposites. Privately, Poe dismissed the idea that the story affirmed the soul's immortality, and he underscored the finality of death: "One point I have not fully carried out—I should have intimated that the *will* did not perfect its intention—there should have been a relapse—a final one—and Ligeia (who had only succeeded in so much as to convey an idea of the truth to the narrator) should be at length entombed as Rowena—the body alterations have gradually faded away." Notwithstanding Poe's omission, the tale as published hardly implies a joyous or lasting reunion; apart from "Eleonora," he rigorously resisted any idealizing of the death of the Other.

What then is the meaning of the apparently supernatural return staged in the separation paradigm? In "Morella" Poe intimates that the reincarnation completes a curse; Morella warns the narrator, "thy days shall be days of sorrow . . . thou shalt bear about with thee thy shroud on earth," perhaps as retribution for the contempt she has received from him. The return of Madeline Usher also savors of revenge; after a bloody and "bitter struggle" to escape her tomb, she destroys the brother who had buried her prematurely, bearing him to the floor "a corpse, and a victim to the terrors he had anticipated." The return of Ligeia seems to victimize Rowena rather than the narrator, but we must remember that, unlike Eleonora, Ligeia never sanctions or encourages her husband's remarriage. Note the avoidance in the gesture by which she signals her reappearance to the narrator: "*Shrinking from my touch,* she let fall from her head the ghastly cerements which had confined it" (italics mine). The point is subtle but important, for we see that the parting marks an irreversible alienation, to which the horrific reunion bears witness. The ultimate implication of the separation model becomes clear: death makes us strangers to each other. In Poe's fiction, the dramatized return of the Other also suggests, paradoxically, that human ties continue to exert a claim and that loss haunts us in the midst of life. If the death of a beautiful woman grants a certain immunity to Poe's protagonist (dissolution is what happens to someone else), the very task of watching and waiting intensifies the consciousness of his own mortality and destroys his hold upon life and reason. Only in "Eleonora" does the narrator accept the death of the Other and commune happily with her spirit. But that situation more nearly resembles a fourth figuration of human destiny.

Transformation. In his 1844 tour de force, "The Premature Burial," Poe wrote, "the boundaries which divide Life from Death, are at best shadowy and vague." Describing one of those "cessations . . . of vitality" known to result in accidental burial, he mused, "where, meantime, was the soul?" The question of the soul's whereabouts during sleep and after death has a long tradition in Western philosophy, stretching back to Plato and Aristotle. But this enigma aroused profound uncertainty for Poe's generation, as gathering religious doubt inevitably came to center on the problem of mortality. The traditional notion of an immortal, individual essence had come under attack from two fronts. Developing medical knowledge had by the early nineteenth century charted the human anatomy so precisely that the venerable belief in a physical seat of the soul (held by Descartes, for example, who exalted the pineal gland) could no longer be sustained. Indeed, skepticism about the soul's very existence increased in direct ratio to physiological understanding. Meanwhile, the Romantic movement, influenced by German idealism, had popularized a transcendental view of man and nature: a world suffused by an Over-Soul that animated human beings (as it did all living things) but that returned unto itself at death, bearing no trace of personal essence. In the face of these popular ideologies, belief in an individuated soul persisted, mainly because that concept was bound up with the individualism that had undergirded Western culture since the early Renaissance. But the apparent failure of religious dogma channeled belief in the soul into secular occultism, both organized and informal.

Matters of death and the soul were never very far from Poe's thoughts. As we have seen, his writing emphasizes the physiological and psychological aspects of dying, suggesting his greater responsiveness to the threat of oblivion than to the prospect of an afterlife. Yet in early poems like *Al Aaraaf* and "Israfel" (as well as tales like "Eleonora"), he could occasionally entertain fancies of transcendence. In a series of four works, which began with "The Conversation of Eiros and Charmion" and ended with "The Power of Words," Poe depicted death as metamorphosis and through supernatural dialogues projected scenes of spiritual reunion and cosmic discovery. In "The Colloquy of Monos and Una," the transformation of the title entities makes possible a retrospective view of death and burial, in which the "evil hour" of separation now appears as a "passage through the dark Valley and Shadow" toward "Life Eternal": a rebirth. After delivering a harangue on earthly problems, Monos relates the "weird narrative" of his own decease, noting the sensory impressions of his last moments, the lamentations of his survivors, preparations for his burial, and the interment itself. He insists that the "breathless and motionless torpor" which was "termed Death by those who stood around [him]" did not deprive him of "sentience." But gradually his senses dim, and Monos becomes aware of a new mode of consciousness, the "sentiment of *duration*," which he terms "the first obvious and certain step of the intemporal soul upon the threshold of the temporal Eternity." Finally the "consciousness of being" yields to a simple sense of place: "The narrow space immediately surrounding what had been the body, was now growing to be the body itself." In reporting this transformation, Poe propounds the idea that the soul and body do not separate at death, that the spirit remains within the mortal frame, still in effect a prisoner of sensation, until the process of decay reduces the body to dust. Yet Poe's final, troubling sentence implies that not even the soul survives this disintegration; what remains is pure absence, "nothingness." But we have the dialogue itself as evidence of an "immortality." Poe appears to suggest that the total annihilation of body and soul must take place before the rebirth or transformation alluded to at the beginning of the work. The self must endure "many lustra" of decomposition ("corrosive hours") before reaching the condition of nullity preliminary to "Life Eternal."

This vision of infinity becomes somewhat clearer in "Mesmeric Revelation." Here the dialogue occurs between Vankirk, a patient dying of tuberculosis, and P., the narrator-mesmerist. On the point of death, Vankirk summons P. to place him in a sleep-waking state, so that he may explore his own "psychal impressions" about the soul. Articulating what may have been Poe's own uncertainties, the dying man admits, "I need not tell you how sceptical I have hitherto been on the topic of the soul's immortality. I cannot deny that there has always existed, as if in that very soul which I have been denying, a vague half-sentiment of its own existence." Under mesmeric influence, and speaking (in the latter portion of the tale) from the beyond, Vankirk elaborates a transcendental theory of God as an all-pervasive spirit, of which the human being is an individualized expression. He affirms of man, "Divested of his corporate investiture, he were God. . . . But he can never be thus divested—at least never *will* be— else we must imagine an action of God returning upon itself—a purposeless and futile action." According to this hypothesis, each of us is trapped within a body that is coextensive with and inseparable from the soul. How then do we escape the tomb? Here is the key to Poe's theory of immortality (and the concept of death as transformation): "There are two bodies—the rudimental and the complete; corresponding with the two conditions of the worm and the butterfly. What we call 'death,' is but the painful metamorphosis. Our present incarnation is progressive, preparatory, temporary. Our future is perfected, ultimate, immortal. The ultimate life is the full design." If we understand "present incarnation" to encompass both flesh and spirit, the metaphysics of "The Colloquy of Monos and Una" becomes intelligible. The temporal body falls away like a chrysalis, revealing the intemporal, "complete" body, the astral body. But Poe is no systematic thinker; in "Mesmeric Revelation" he drops the idea of a season in limbo (called "the alloted days of stupor" in "The Conversation of Eiros and Charmion") and says that "at death or metamorphosis, these creatures, enjoying the ultimate life—immortality" inhabit "SPACE itself" as "non-entities" invisible to the angels. Unfortunately, the final tale in the sequence, "The Power of Words," sheds no light on these mysteries, defining the soul merely as a "thirst" for ultimate knowledge.

These philosophical inconsistencies are perhaps beside the point. What seems significant about the cycle of spiritualized dialogues is Poe's inclination to see body and soul as inextricably bonded. Despite the conception of an unearthly, astral form, an odd materialism informs Poe's notion of the spirit world; "Aidenn" is simply a place where things, substances, are less densely constituted. God is "unparticled matter," souls have bodies, and words have a physical power." It is as if, for all of his mystical inclinations, Poe cannot escape an empirical vision of a bounded world. His depiction of an afterlife seems to express a yearning for a realm "out of space, out of time," beyond the contingencies of mortal existence. Yet in fact his spirit figures carry with them a good deal of earthly baggage—memories, affections, beliefs, political opinions—and spend much of their time (if one can thus speak of the eternal) reflecting upon personal experiences or explaining celestial phenomena according to mundane scientific principles. In short, Poe's visionary texts (and here I include the monumentally confused *Eureka*) project a false transcendence, a phantasmic existence after death, conceptually embedded in a cosmos of matter and energy, a system that culminates in irreversible dissolution: entropy.

V

Among Poe's manifold representations of death and dying, we discern no single formulation that might confidently be described as the essential design. His object as a writer was not, of course, to construct a programmatic analysis of human fate; his thematic diversity and penchant for irony complicate even further an identification of his "real" conceptual matrix. Nevertheless, the imagery of death recurs with such insistence that its imaginative priority seems self-evident. Edward Davidson once described Poe as a "verbal landscapist of death," and in an early poem, "The City in the Sea," we encounter the characteristic scene of silence and desolation, upon which "Death looks gigantically down." For Poe, death was indeed gigantic, not in crude physical terms but as a ubiquitous and oppressive presence. Personal experience, popular culture, and intellectual history conspired to make it so. The pathetic facts of his own life—the successive deaths of his parents, his surrogate mother (Mrs. Jane Stith Standard), his foster mother (Mrs. Allan), and his child bride, Virginia—describe a pattern of loss that must have haunted him like a specter. His inveterate melancholy also fed upon the funereal spirit of the age, as manifested in the sentimental offerings of the gift books and ladies' magazines. And his fear and trembling (to use the phrase of his contemporary, Kierkegaard) further derived from the crisis of authority and understanding that shook Western culture in the eighteenth century. Among other consequences, this crisis seriously challenged or destroyed traditional ways of accepting death and introduced a welter of new, secular conceptions that necessarily contributed further uncertainty. To use the phrase of Becker, it was at this moment that the "eclipse of secure communal ideologies of redemption" produced the anxiety characteristic of the modern age. Since 1700 rapidly changing conceptions of death, symptomatic of a decentered culture, have failed to mitigate or resolve the underlying dread. It it a mark of Poe's genius that he perceived the central problem of death and sensed in his own dubiety the confusion of our existential plight. As Sarah Helen Whitman shrewdly perceived in 1859, the "unrest and faithlessness of the age culminated in him"; Poe was the saddest and loneliest writer of his generation because he "came to sound the very depths of the abyss," to plumb the nature of modern despair.

No story in the Poe canon sounds the depths more effectively than "The Facts in the Case of M. Valdemar," a tale that incorporates elements of all four models previously discussed. A sequel to "Mesmeric Revelation," "Valdemar" further illuminates the disjunction between body and soul as disclosed by mesmeric experiment; it postulates the threshold experience of a man *in articulo mortis*. Like the tales of separation, it portrays mortality as an object of scrutiny; the narrator furnishes expert observations on the physiological decline of his friend. Like characters in the tales of compulsion, M. Valdemar expresses the desire for death ("Do not wake me—let me die so") and longs for release from the mesmeric trance so that his dissolution may be completed. The ensuing spectacle of immediate putrefaction ties the story to the annihilation model and exemplifies the naturalistic horror inherent in death. This is not to suggest that "Valdemar" involves a conscious manipulation of these patterns; rather, the synthetic, composite effect seems the result of an intense concentration of anxiety, a focusing, as it were, of Poe's ambivalent perceptions of mortality.

Despite the fact that Poe in correspondence acknowledged the tale to be a "hoax," "Valdemar" demands serious attention as a conceptualization of death. With excruciating precision, it records the grotesque "facts" of the protagonist's apparent demise:

> The eyes rolled themselves slowly open, the pupils disappearing upwardly; the skin generally assumed a cadaverous hue, resembling not so much parchment as white paper; and the circular

> hectic spots which, hitherto, had been strongly defined in the
> center of each cheek, *went out* at once. . . . The upper lip, at the
> same time, writhed itself away from the teeth, which it had
> previously covered completely; while the lower jaw fell upon
> with an audible jerk, leaving the mouth widely extended, and
> disclosing in full view the swollen and blackened tongue.

The disappearance of the "hectic spots" brings to mind, appropriately, the sudden extinction of the sun in "MS. Found in a Bottle," while the revelation of the writhing lip recalls "Metzengerstein," "Berenice," and other Poe tales in which teeth function as a sign of death. This moment of apparent decease has its counterpart in the tale's unforgettable final image, the instantaneous decomposition of Valdemar: "Upon the bed, before that whole company, there lay a nearly liquid mass of loathsome—of detestable putridity." Apart from effecting our revulsion, these details serve a figurative purpose, for "Valdemar" dramatizes the scientific effort—undertaken in the eighteenth century and continuing in our era of medical technology—to understand, control, and perhaps finally conquer the major causes of death. From an empirical viewpoint, cessation of life results from physiological processes that can theoretically be halted or reversed. Even aging has proved susceptible to retardation, and recent developments in genetic engineering and organ replacement bring ever closer the possibility of a technologically guaranteed immortality. However improbable or undesirable this idea seems, one can scarcely deny that the great dream of our scientific utopia lies in the direction of extending life beyond its traditional limits and converting death into a manageable, discretionary experience. Like Hawthorne's Dr. Rappaccini, the narrator of "Valdemar" uses scientific (or pseudoscientific) methods to control the processes of life artificially. His ultimate object is to determine "to what extent, or for how long a period, the encroachments of Death might be arrested" by mesmerism. The stratagem succeeds in postponing Valdemar's dissolution, but when the man is awakened from his vegetative stupor, the grotesque final scene betrays the limitation of human efficacy and reaffirms the sovereignty of death. In effect, the illusion of a scientifically insured immortality disintegrates with Valdemar.

Another key to the symbolic ramifications of the tale lies in the supernatural voice, the "harsh, and broken and hollow" sound that seems to emanate from some deep or distant source, producing a "gelatinous" impression. When the voice declares, "I *have been* sleeping—and now—now—*I am dead*," it perpetrates what Roland Barthes has called a "scandal of language, . . . the coupling of the first person (*I*) and of the attribute '*dead*' "; it "asserts two contraries at the same time (Life, Death)"; and it effects a "scandalous return to the literal" when "Death, as primordial repressed, erupts directly into language." The last point seems especially pertinent: the tale violates language, logic, and cultural taboo, allowing the unspeakable to speak, the unbearable sight to be seen. It compels us to confront death in all of its visceral repulsiveness, unsoftened by the effusion of sentiment or the prospect of a spiritual afterlife.

As noted earlier, Poe rejected the illusion of "the Beautiful Death" which beguiled his generation, and through the preternatural voice in "Valdemar" he expresses the hard physical and psychological truth at the core of modern consciousness. In this work as in so many others, supernaturalism intrudes upon the world of reason and experience to deliver the message of mortality. The uncanny produces a disruption, shatters the illusion of one's control over the flow of existence; it rivets the consciousness of Poe's protagonists like the first undeniable sign of a mortal illness. It arrives as a threat to the quest for knowledge, beauty, and godlike dominance, driving home a perception of the existential paradox summarized by Becker: "Man is literally split in two: he has an awareness of his own splendid uniqueness in that he sticks out of nature with a towering majesty, and yet he goes back into the ground a few feet in order blindly and dumbly to rot and disappear forever. It is a terrifying dilemma to be in and to have to live with." While Poe could entertain visions of transcendence, he was finally too much the victim of our own crisis of death to exorcise its dread. Yet he faced the "terrifying dilemma" with remarkable tenacity and acuity, producing a literature that seems, in our age of "invisible death," more than ever disturbing and menacing. Little wonder that for many, Poe cannot be taken seriously: to do so is to confront the fearful yet vitalizing truth that our century has done its best to deny.

Poe's Narrative Monologues

Ken Frieden

Edgar Allan Poe's narrative monologues border on madness and disrupt the normally associated conventions of voice. Monologue is solitary speech, whether physically isolated, morally deviant, or semantically opaque; Poe's strongest narrators are not only solitary human beings, for as a fictive consequence of the criminal acts they narrate, they often speak from solitary confinement. But while his narrators appear isolated and deviant, Poe's narratives themselves swerve away from norms. An initial problem is to distinguish between the narrative conventions Poe borrows, transforms, and creates, because the superficially popular genre of his fiction conceals the relationship to English literary tradition. By emphasizing the intensity of reader experience above all else, Poe himself neglects literary history, yet even the most emotionally charged reception of a text is made possible by literary context. Although Poe does respond to conventions of the Gothic novel, his revision of epistolary narrative and conversational poetry is more decisive.

Poe's most compelling fictions succeed as representations of diverse and often pathological characters. Yet if we suspect that consciousness, in literature, is "a fictive appearance generated by language, rather than something language describes or reflects," then we must attend to the devices by which fiction creates the illusion of representing a consciousness. Such devices depend on intertextual relations in literary history. The "I" emerges at various stages and in all genres of English literature, including dramatic

From *Genius and Monologue*. © 1985 by Cornell University. Cornell University Press, 1985.

soliloquy, conversational poetry, and first-person narrative. Whereas the dramatic frame clarifies what it means for a character to say "I," the poetic and narrative "I" raises problems that derive from the disparity between the actual form of writing and the imaginary scene of speaking. Poe revises the conversational mode to present dreams, fantasies, passions, obsessions.

The meaning of first-person narrative in stories by Poe becomes clearer in the context of his eighteenth-century precursors. The earliest epistolary fiction of Samuel Richardson brings the narrator into a peculiar condition of identity with the narrated world. If the surest truth of experience is "I think," the most irrefutable literary assertion is "I write." Yet who is the "I" of such a statement? The fictional "I" creates itself and, simultaneously, its frame. Especially where the letters of only one character constitute a fictional world, there is no clear separation between the narrating persona and the world narrated. After Richardson, then, the scene of writing is an accepted component of the English novel. This scene influences the later development of self-conscious prose and particularly modern internal monologue that pretends to reproduce a scene of unwritten thoughts.

Prior narrative traditions are tame, however, when compared with those introduced by Poe's first-person tales. In a sense, Poe transfers the intensely present "I" of Romantic verse to an analogous "I" of narrative. But his first-person accounts do not merely transpose the conversation poem into a narrative form: Poe's narrated monologues unsettle the representational conventions on which they initially depend. At the same time that a first-person voice reveals exalted states of consciousness, Poe subverts the realistic pretense by focusing attention on the act of writing. The scene of Poe's greatest originality is the point at which he disrupts the conversational tradition by tampering with the unexamined illusion of narrative voice.

"I WRITE IN THE PRESENT TENSE"

Apart from the obvious, yet superficial, influence of Gothic novels, Poe is most significantly influenced by the first-person form of epistolary fiction. A first-person "voice" is clearly essential to the genre based on personal letters and diary entries.

Samuel Richardson innovates in a monological vein by producing the epistolary novel *Pamela* (1740). Twentieth-century literary norms make the novelty of Richardson's narrative devices difficult to appreciate: Richardson introduces a genre of self-reflective writing while planting the seeds of its undoing. Early in *Pamela,* for example, the heroine represents her past thoughts in a letter to her parents: "O Pamela, said I to myself, why art thou so foolish and fearful? Thou hast done no harm! What, if thou fearest an unjust judge, when thou art innocent, would'st thou do before a just one, if thou wert guilty? Have courage, Pamela, thou knowest the worst! . . . So I cheered myself; but yet my poor heart sunk, and my spirits were quite broken." Recalling her thoughts in the form of a pseudodialogue at a specific moment, Pamela apparently practices what Shaftesbury calls the "Home-*Dialect* of *Soliloquy*." As Shaftesbury's analysis predicts, the soliloquist becomes "two distinct *Persons*" when Pamela reasons with herself. At the height of perplexity she contemplates suicide and thinks: "Pause here a little, Pamela, on what thou art about, before thou takest the dreadful leap; and consider whether there be no way yet left, no hope, if not to escape from this wicked house, yet from the mischiefs threatened thee in it." On one level, this passage works as psychological realism that represents a process of thought. At the same time, the pause in Pamela's thoughts is a pause in her narrative of events, like the dramatic monologue Diderot describes as "a moment of repose for the action, and of turmoil for the character." While these passages represent past thoughts, the narrative form appears to correspond to the represented moment.

Richardson's Pamela also shows a self-conscious awareness of the process of writing. She accounts for her possession of writing materials and at several points notes her time of composition to the hour. Pamela's activity of writing is, in addition, occasionally interrupted by the world she describes. Amid contemplations, Pamela writes, "But I must break off; here's somebody coming." Even more vividly, she writes of her feeling of dread and its influence on writing: "Though I dread to see him, yet do I wonder I have not . . . I can hardly write; yet, as I can do nothing else, I know not how to forbear!—Yet I cannot hold my pen—How crooked and trembling the lines!—I must leave off, till I can get quieter fingers!—" After Pamela describes her inability to write, the narrative breaks. As the fictional Pamela exists only by virtue of her writing, she literally "can do nothing else." Her peculiar self-awareness only slightly disturbs the representational illusion with the recognition that "Pamela" exists only as a fictive writer. We experience Pamela primarily as a writer, but she remains a realistic character within the fiction.

Richardson's novel explicitly narrates Mr. B's approach to Pamela, and it tells a parallel tale of the reader's approach to her texts. Mr. B must fight to obtain Pamela's writings, a struggle which identifies him with the reader, who now holds the texts that are also objects within the fictional world. Like a sympathetic reader, Mr. B understands and loves Pamela all the more for the words she pens; in fact, he only begins to acknowledge the depth of her character through her writing, just as the reader discovers her.

"I write, therefore I am" is the principle of first-person narration. Even for Mr. B, Pamela is most truly herself in her writings. Yet as Mr. B kidnaps and isolates her, she is pushed toward a mode of writing that is not intended to be read. Pamela cherishes the notion that she can be identical with what she writes and defends herself against charges of insincerity: "I know I write my heart; and that is not deceitful." The purity of her manuscripts at first depends on their remaining untouched by Mr. B; when he demands to see all she writes, he undermines the very possibility of writing. Pamela imagines that she will no longer be able to write "with any face"— or heart?—if she must write without monological isolation, in the expectation of Mr. B's readership. In a sense, then, the novel ought to end as soon as she and Mr. B are united; Pamela writes, of necessity, for only as long as they are separated and she contemplates matters that she must hide from him. The scene of writing is linked to the developments that overcome Pamela's solitude by bringing her closer to the reader and to Mr. B.

Henry Fielding proves to be a genuine critic when he subsequently lambastes the new epistolary fiction in his *Shamela* (1741), revealing the essence of Richardson's narrative monologues by means of comic distortions. *Shamela* does not merely parody *Pamela*'s more obvious quirks, such as the ambiguous character of the heroine. Fielding's caricature pokes fun at the improbable narrative device by which Pamela continues to write during the most heated moments of action, and in so doing, Fielding reveals the nature of Richardson's epistolary form.

One of Shamela's most humorous diary entries, purportedly written "Thursday Night, Twelve o'Clock," may serve as an introduction to Poe's revision of narrative conventions. In a style that obliquely prepares the way for Molly Bloom's internal monologue, Shamela describes events as they occur:

> Mrs. Jervis and I are just in bed, and the door unlocked; if my master should come—Odsbobs! I hear him just coming in at the door. You see I write in the present tense, as Parson Williams says. Well, he is in bed between us, we both shamming a sleep; he steals his hand into my bosom, which I, as if in my sleep, press close to me with mine, and then pretend to awake.—I no sooner see him, but I scream out to Mrs. Jervis, she feigns likewise but just to come to herself; we both begin, she to becall, and I to bescratch very liberally. After having made a pretty free use of my fingers, without any great regard to the parts I attacked, I counterfeit a swoon.

Shamela is a counterfeiter both in bed and in her narrative pretense that suggests simultaneity with narrated action. She can as easily feign an impossible narrative stance as she can "counterfeit a swoon." Thus the parody of Pamela's character combines with a comic exaggeration of her manner of writing: Fielding exposes the possibly bizarre consequences of Richardson's innovation. First-person, present-tense writing results in a variety of difficulties, such as the paradoxical illusion that Shamela can simultaneously write her diary and engage in a battle with Mr. B. Nothing in *Pamela* reaches such self-contradictory extremes, of course, yet Fielding aptly captures the potential turns of perversity made possible by Richardson's representations of thought and of moments of writing. One hundred years later, E. A. Poe develops a kindred genre in which diabolical monologists appear menacingly present.

"Why Will You Say That I Am Mad?"

In one sense, then, Poe's first-person narrators stand firmly in the tradition of epistolary fiction as initiated by Richardson and parodied by Fielding. But when Poe situates his work in relation to tradition, he refers most exclusively to poetic models. In "The Poetic Principle," Poe establishes both an aesthetic theory and a canon of "English and American poems which best suit my taste." While Poe argues strongly that he has discerned *the* poetic principle, he describes something that he himself invents, in connection with his own poetic preferences. Poe favors short poems of high intensity, on the basis of a "peculiar principle" of psychology:

> a poem deserves its title only inasmuch as it excites, by elevating the soul. The value of the poem is in the ration of this elevating excitement. But all excitements are, through a psychal necessity, transient. That degree of excitement which would entitle a poem to be so called at all, cannot be sustained throughout a composition of any great length. After the lapse of half an hour, at the very utmost, it flags—fails—a revulsion ensues—and then the poem is, in effect, and in fact, no longer such.

On the surface, Poe's principle of literary taste is a "psychal necessity," the human inability to sustain a state of excitement for longer than half an hour. Imposing a half-hour limit is not literally necessary, Poe imagines a faintly sexual scene, derived from figurative demands of a literary scene in which the excitement "flags—fails—a revulsion ensues," and the poem loses its status as poem. An emotional coupling between poem and reader takes place. But does the poetic principle really derive from "psychal necessity," or does poetry control psychology? Only superficially do Poe's poetics depend on exclusively psychological principles. If Poe admires verses that produce an exalted state in the mind of the reader, he seeks poetic personae that create illusions of similarly exalted conditions.

The poetic principle of elevating excitement produces a present scene analogous to that of Coleridge's convesational poetry. A moment in the speaker's experience corresponds to the reader's exalted experience. One mode of Poe's writing is, then, a radicalization of the poetic genre Coleridge begins with "The Eolian Harp." In his "Letter to B——," he admires Coleridge's "towering intellect" and "gigantic power" yet adds that "in reading that man's poetry, I tremble like one who stands upon a volcano, conscious from the very darkness bursting from the crater, of the fire and the light that are weltering below." Whereas Coleridge "imprisoned his own conceptions," Poe—for the sake of an exalted half hour—strives to free the bound forces, as in "Tamerlane," the dream poems, "The Raven," "The Sleeper," and "Annabel Lee." Poe's tales present even more powerful first-person presences. Often enough, Poe's narrators are themselves imprisoned, yet in some way liberated by the scene of narration. The liberation of bound forces and representation of an exalted consciousness are initial premises for Poe's fiction. Poe gives free expression to *thanatos,* an impulse toward death or destruction; beyond their scenes of murder, Poe's narrators perform their own self-destruction in dramas linked to "the imp of the preverse."

The deviant narrators of "The Tell-Tale Heart," "The Black Cat," and "The Imp of the Perverse" in some ways extend into short fiction the epistolary and conversational modes developed by Richardson, Coleridge, and their followers. Yet Poe's narrators often confront the representational illusion at the same time that they dispute the superficial claim that they are insane. In Poe's texts, the scene of madness combines with a controlled scene of writing; at exactly this point, Poe destabilizes the genre he assumes: rhetorical forms both constitute and question a conversational pretense.

On one level, Poe's mad monologues may be read as expressions of psychological realism. "The Tell-Tale Heart," for example, presents itself as the spontaneous narrative of a murderer: "True!—nervous—very, very dreadful nervous I had been and am! but why *will* you say that I am mad? The disease had sharpened my senses—not destroyed—not dulled them. Above all was the sense of hearing acute. I heard all things in the heaven and in the earth. I heard many things in hell. How, then, am I mad? Hearken! and observe how healthily—how calmly I can tell you the whole story."

As the scene of discourse, we may imagine ourselves in conversation with a confined lunatic. His denial of madness only intensifies the effect of his bizarre claim to have "heard all things in the heaven and in the earth." The opening words imply that we have provoked the speaker by asserting what he denies: far from being insane, he says, "the disease had sharpened my senses," and if we choose to listen, we will share his exalted mood for a few minutes. As soon as we begin to read, then, we find ourselves written into a drama in which we have accused the speaker of being nervous or mad. The narrative opens with a paradox, however, which unsettles the representational illusion. The speaker combines mad assertions with narrative lucidity and presents a disconcerting contradiction between his representing and represented personae. The discrepancy between sane narrator and madman perhaps shows the error of assuming that linguistic normalcy implies psychological normalcy. The narrator is mad, or at least abnormal, according to his own account, because he kills an old man for no reason. He is doubly mad when he imagines he hears the pounding of the dead man's heart and gives away the crime he had concealed. Yet the narrator tells a coherent tale, as if to demonstrate out of spite that he is sane, refuting the ordinary belief that he must be mad. This contradiction overturns mimetic conventions: a literal reading of the mad narrator shows itself to be naive, because only Poe's textual pretense creates the illusion of disparity between madman and sane narrator.

"The Black Cat" follows similar patterns, without the exclamatory wildness of the tell-tale narration. The contradiction is even sharper in "the most wild yet most homely narrative which I am about to pen," for the scene of writing is explicit. Condemned to death, the narrator explains: "To-morrow I die, and to-day I would unburthen my soul. My immediate purpose is to place before the world, plainly, succinctly, and without comment, a series of mere household events. In their consequences, these events have terrified—have tortured—have destroyed me. Yet I will not attempt to expound them." Again Poe invents a situation of radical conflict, in which lurid and lucid details compete. Renouncing all value judgments, the narrator resolves to tell his tale in the most indifferent tones. He explains his peculiar behavior only by reference to a philosophical principle. The speaker has been prone to mysterious states, as when "the fury of a demon instantly possessed me"; the narrator attributes his ultimate downfall to perversity:

Of this spirit philosophy takes no account. Yet I am not more sure that my soul lives, than I am that perverseness is one of the primitive impulses of the human heart—one of the indivisible primary faculties, or sentiments, which give direction to the character of Man. Who has not, a hundred times, found himself committing a vile or a silly action, for no other reason than because he knows he should *not*? Have we not a perpetual inclination, in the teeth of our best judgment, to violate that which is *Law*, merely because we understand it to be such?

Similar to an evil genius, the "spirit of perverseness" appears as a reversal of the *daimonion* that turns Socrates away from evil. The spirit of perverseness inverts, turns upside down, subverts: "It was this unfathomable longing of the soul to *vex itself*—to offer violence to its own nature—to do wrong for the wrong's sake only—that urged me to continue and finally to consummate the injury I had inflicted upon the unoffending brute." Rather than speak of some psychological drive that leads men to evil, the narrator points to an abstract, counterrational impulse to violate whatever is—nature or law. The impulse to perverseness, governed by the rhetorical figure of chiasmus, is a kind of hidden nature in man. The mad narrator undoes himself both through his perverse actions and in his submerged story of textual subversion, a tribute to "the power of words." The spirit of perverseness is an anti-*daimonion* that turns the speaker against himself; the overt instigator, a black cat, bears the name of Pluto, god of the underworld.

"The Imp of the Perverse" reveals more explicitly the perverse power of words. Half treatise and half tale, the text opens in the tone of philosophical inquiry: "In the consideration of the faculties and impulses—of the *prima mobilia* of the human soul, the phrenologists have failed to make room for a propensity which, although obviously existing as a radical, primitive, irreducible sentiment, has been equally overlooked by all the moralists who have preceded them. In the pure arrogance of the reason, we have all overlooked it." The neglected primum mobile resists the efforts of reason, of perception, of human purpose. Speaking in the tones of rationality, Poe's narrator points to the limits of reason, beyond which our sesnses must be guided by belief. Experiencing vertigo on the edge of an abyss, we encounter "a shape, far more terrible than any genius or any demon of a tale." A thought takes form: "Because our reason violently deters us from the brink, *therefore* do we the most impetuously approach it." Rather than call us away from evil, the perverted "genius" presses us toward the abyss. The perverse further opposes reason and systems of good and evil because it can at least appear to "operate in furtherance of good."

The narrator condenses the paradoxical perverseness into a definition: "It is, in fact, a *mobile* without motive, a motive not *motivirt* (sic)." Displacing comfortable theological beliefs according to which God is the primum mobile, this alternative, an introjected "mobile without motive," upsets all order. The perverse suggests that there can be motion without any rational ground, and even the apparent motive can be without motivation.

By a perverse logic, the entire analytical discourse is transformed when the speaker describes his present situation. Not only does the apparently unmotivated take on motive; perversely, we become visitors to a prison rather than readers of a philosophical discourse:

> I have said thus much, that in some measure I may answer your question, that I may explain to you why I am here, that I may assign to you something that shall have at last the faint aspect of a cause for my wearing these fetters, and for my tenanting this cell of the condemned. Had I not been thus prolix, you might either have misunderstood me altogether; or, with the rabble, have fancied me mad. As it is, you will easily perceive that I am one of the many uncounted victims of the Imp of the Perverse.

The speaker denies his madness by calling himself a victim of the principle he has outlined. Yet his language hovers between calculation and illogic. The narrator explains "why I am here . . . wearing these fetters" by reference to a cause that is only a perverse absence of cause. From the standpoint of realistic representation, the perverse narrator betrays his deviance through linguistic peculiarities. He begins his tale: "It is impossible that any deed could have been wrought with a more thorough deliberation. For weeks, for months, I pondered upon the means of the murder." Like the narrator of "The Tell-Tale Heart" who comments that "it is impossible to say how first the idea entered my brain," he assumes an understanding of what he has not yet explained. Both fictional speakers break accepted conventions by employing the definite article, where "*the* idea" and "*the* murder" have not been previously explicated. If we read these narrators as mimetic characters, their linguistic deviations may be signs of defective mental processes. From another prospective, however, ill-formed syntax is a contradiction embedded in the narrative by Poe, to enhance the contradictions in the narrator's account.

The narrator undoes himself in a scene of internalized self-address, after the words "I am safe" have become his standard refrain: "One day, whilst sauntering along the streets, I arrested myself in the act of murmuring, half aloud, these customary syllables. In a fit of petulance, I remodelled them thus; 'I am safe—I am safe—yes—if I be not fool enough to make open confession!' " Language overthrows him, for as soon as he asserts one thing, the perverse drives him to subvert this rational thesis:

> No sooner had I spoken those words, than I felt an icy chill creep to my heart. I had had some experience in these fits of perversity, (whose nature I have been at some trouble to explain), and I remembered well, that in no instance, I had successfully resisted their attacks. And now my own casual self-suggestion that I might possibly be fool enough to confess the murder of which I had been guilty, confronted me, as if the very ghost of him whom I had murdered—and beckoned me on to death.

A rhetorical moment takes the place of all ghosts, when "the imp of the perverse" drives the speaker to confess. "The rabble" would understand his behavior as a symptom of madness, but his perversity turns out to be a reflex inherent in words.

"MS. FOUND IN A BOTTLE"

Poe's radical revision of the conversational pretense derives, then, not from the poetic principle of psychological exaltation, but from a rhetorical application of the spirit of perverseness. The mad monologues achieve powerful effects of psychological realism and can be read as the conversations of deranged speakers. Beyond the operation of perverseness in self-destructive behavior, however, Poe's narrators show that language may undermine its own theses. As soon as a murderer tells himself, "I am safe—yes—if I be not fool enough to make open confession," he already assures that he will pronounce his doom. In the tradition of the epistolary and confessional novel, several of Poe's short fictions more radically disrupt the conversational mode by recognizing themselves as writing, and the realistic pretense fades.

"MS. Found in a Bottle" initially confronts the reader with an uncertainty: Is *this* the manuscript found, or will it describe a recovery of some other document in a bottle? The manuscript we read is not, in any obvious sense, found in a bottle. Apparently, the story may be *about* a "MS. Found in a Bottle," or it may actually *be* this manuscript. The story generates the odd illusion that it exists within itself. A perplexing ambiguity makes impossible any clear distinction between the text that represents and the text that is represented. Midway through the narrative, we are informed: "It was no long while ago that I ventured into the captain's own private cabin, and took thence the materials with which I write, and have written. I shall from time to time continue this journal. It is true that I may not find an opportunity of transmitting it to the world, but I will not fail to make the endeavor. At the last moment I will enclose the MS. in a bottle, and cast it within the sea." The bottle is a familiar figure of textuality, of the metonymic relation between form and content, literary container and the thing contained. But the expected configuration is inverted: whereas the container is a bottle within the textual world, what is contained is the text itself. This illusion is also destroyed, however, because the bottle only exists by virtue of the text "inside" that describes its existence. Perversely, the text of "MS. Found in a Bottle" usurps the world it describes by showing that it is identical with that world. The mimetic convention slips away when the text discloses itself merely as a text; the bottle and the wine merge, the container and the contained become inseparable.

Yet the representational level remains: "At the last moment I will enclose the MS. in a bottle, and cast it within the sea." The text masquerades as an object in the world it represents; Poe, by titling the story, pretends to verify this pretense. Poe also "adds" an epigraph that accords a special status to the words of the desperate writer: "Qui n'a plus qu'un moment à vivre / N'a plus rien à dissimuler" ("One who has only a moment to live / Has nothing more to conceal"). According to this proverb, then, no dissimulation can occur if the writer is on the verge of death. In the final lines of the story, "amid a roaring, and bellowing, and thundering of ocean and tempest," the narrator writes that "the ship is quivering—oh God! and—going down!" At this moment, presumably, the text is enclosed in the bottle, just as the ship is swallowed up by the sea. But the representational illusion is also engulfed as the moment of writing becomes the moment of death: we can never remove the text from its alleged bottle, for text and bottle are identical. According to the rhetorical figure, the inside of the bottle should represent its contained meanings, but the fullest meaning of Poe's story is that this text is identical with its inside, the entire text is its meaning, so that in some sense the bottle can never be uncorked.

The writer or speaker in "The Cask of Amontillado" never reveals his present place, yet he embeds figurative clues within the tale he narrates. In connection with the story of ruthless murder, a first level of allegory makes the unfortunate Fortunato a stand-in for the reader. As readers, our mistake is to think we can confidently, safely uncork a text and savor its wine. Within the representational illusion, Fortunato shows the same *faiblesse:*

"He had a weak point—this Fortunato—although in other regards he was a man to be respected and even feared. He prided himself on his connoisseurship in wine." The narrator rightly claims that "I did not differ from him materially"—because, of course, both are textual fictions— "and bought largely whenever I could." Yet they do differ: Fortunato prides himself on an ability at wine tasting; the narrator represents himself primarily as a buyer of wines. Fortunato is like a presumptuous literary critic, while Montressor is a writer who stores his textual bottles in endless vaults. While staging Fortunato's death, the narrator figures himself as a writer within the story. Fortunato makes the mistake of wishing to outdo Luchresi, who is reputed to have a fine "critical turn."

As he walks unknowingly toward his tomb, Fortunato laughs and "threw the bottle upward with a gesticulation I did not understand." This is a potentially troubling moment for the narrator, whose reader has taken the text, or the act of signifying, into his own hands:

> I looked at him in surprise. He repeated the movement—a grotesque one.
> "You do not comprehend?" he said.
> "Not I," I replied.
> "Then you are not of the brotherhood."
> "How?"
> "You are not of the masons."

The speaker is troubled by his victim's continued independence. How can the author of a text or scheme respond to such a rebellion? At this provocation, which is like that of an elusive reader, the narrator turns the situation around:

> "You are not of the masons."
> "Yes, yes," I said; "yes, yes."
> "You? Impossible! A mason?"
> "A mason," I replied.
> "A sign," he said.
> "It is this," I answered, producing a trowel from beneath the folds of my *roquelaire*.
> "You jest," he exclaimed, recoiling a few paces.

At first, "mason" refers to the secret order of Masons, an order that separates itself by means of arcane signs. Yet the narrator quells his reader's rebellion by demonstrating that his signs escape him; we now understand the opening line of the story: "The thousand injuries of Fortunato I had borne as I best could, but when he ventured upon insult, I vowed revenge." Poe's persona takes revenge on his critics, showing their inability to understand what they say by literalizing their figures of speech and demonstrating that their error entombs them. Fortunato believes that the Masonic order controls its secret language, but he learns that its language can control him. The pun on "mason" turns a trowel into an ominously literal sign of the Mason's demise, and Fortunato can only lean heavily on the narrator's arm as he walks toward his death.

"The Cask of Amontillado" suppresses the rebellious reader by writing him into the text and by entombing him in a subterranean vault. The trowel, a figure for the stylus, walls up unfortunate Fortunato, who tries to dismiss Montressor's action as a joke. But the act of writing is utterly serious: as "I forced the last stone into its position; I plastered it up," and the story ends. The Mason, unable to control his trope, finds himself victimized by the perverse action of masonry. The narrator becomes confused with what is narrated, the container with the contained, as if urging us to disbelieve the mimetic conventions that pretend to present the voice of a speaking subject. The reader, too, should be unable to savor his wine, confronted by a double who has become like wine decomposing within a bottle, the corpse within a textual tomb.

Poe takes up the first-person form only to transgress its usual limitations. The "I" no longer rests with a stable representational function, for behind the mask are only contours of the mask. Where the fictionally speaking voice becomes inextricably bound up with the events it speaks, the more solid ground of mimetic fiction crumbles. There remains an enhanced sensitivity to the dynamics of textual illusion.

First-person narratives, from Richardson to Poe, enact the unification of narrator and narrated, narration and event, creator and created. When the mimetic framework is questioned by internal contradictions, self-narrative unsettles the barrier between signifying and referential functions of language. To represent a self, narration reflects itself.

The literary life of self perhaps corresponds to an equally fictional worldly self that depends on performance for its existence. The monos of monologue can no longer stand as a subject or monad and is rather a textual swerve. For monologue is not the *logos* of subjectivity but only the linguistic embodiment of isolation and deviance that reveals perverse origins of the fictive subject.

Chronology

<table>
<tr><td>1809</td><td>Born in Boston, January 19, the second of three children of David Poe and his wife, Elizabeth Arnold, both actors. Poe's father subsequently abandons the family.</td></tr>
<tr><td>1811</td><td>Death of Poe's mother in Richmond, Virginia. The children are taken into different households, Edgar into that of John Allan, a Richmond merchant. Not legally adopted, he is nevertheless renamed Edgar Allan.</td></tr>
<tr><td>1815–20</td><td>Resides with the Allans in Scotland and London.</td></tr>
<tr><td>1820–25</td><td>Educated in private schools, after the Allans return to Virginia.</td></tr>
<tr><td>1826</td><td>Enters University of Virginia (founded by Jefferson the year before), where he studies languages. Gambling debts compel him to leave, after Allan refuses to pay them.</td></tr>
<tr><td>1827</td><td>Enlists in army in Boston, where his first book, Tamerlane and Other Poems, appears and is ignored.</td></tr>
<tr><td>1828–29</td><td>Honorably discharged as sergeant major, Poe lives in Baltimore, where Al Aaraaf, Tamerlane, and Minor Poems is published.</td></tr>
<tr><td>1830–31</td><td>Enters West Point in May 1830; does well in studies but is expelled in January 1831 after deliberately breaking rules. Breach with John Allan. Poems, Second Edition published. Poe lives in Baltimore with his father's sister, Maria Clemm, and her daughter Virginia, then eight years old. His brother, also living with the Clemms, dies in August. Poe begins to write tales.</td></tr>
<tr><td>1832–35</td><td>Tutors cousin Virginia Clemm. A number of the tales appear in various journals. Death of John Allan. Poe writes book reviews and becomes editorial assistant for Southern Literary Messenger. Moves to Richmond with Virginia and Mrs.</td></tr>
</table>

Clemm; becomes editor of the journal, to which he contributes reviews, poems, and stories.

1836   Marries Virginia Clemm, not yet fourteen; her mother stays on as housekeeper.

1837–38   Resigns from the *Messenger* and moves with his household to New York City, where he is unable to secure editorial work. Publishes "Ligeia" and *The Narrative of Arthur Gordon Pym.* Moves to Philadelphia.

1839–40   Works for *Gentleman's Magazine,* where "William Wilson" and "The Fall of the House of Usher" appear. Publishes the two-volume *Tales of the Grotesque and Arabesque* in Philadelphia, late in 1839. After losing his job, he attempts unsuccessfully to found his own magazine.

1841–42   As an editor of *Graham's Magazine,* he prints "The Murders in the Rue Morgue." In January 1842, Virginia Poe suffers severe hemorrhage, never fully recovers.

1843–45   Poe's reputation rises with the prizewinning "The Gold-Bug." Moves to New York City. Despite his lecturing, editing, and extensive publication, Poe is never financially secure. His drinking is increasingly a problem. "The Raven," published in January 1845, is immensely popular. *Tales* published in July 1845, *The Raven and Other Poems* that November. He becomes owner and editor of the *Broadway Journal.*

1846   Abandons *Broadway Journal* because of his depression and financial problems. Moves household to Fordham, New York, where Virginia is cared for by her mother and Marie Louise Shew.

1847   Virginia dies January 30. Poe, himself very ill, is nursed by Mrs. Clemm and Mrs. Shew.

1848   Proposes marriage to the poet Sarah Helen Whitman, who later breaks off the engagement. Publishes *Eureka: A Prose Poem* in June.

1849   A year of rapid decline, marked by heavy drinking and paranoid delusions. Poe travels to Richmond, where he is engaged to Elmira Royster Shelton. Sails to Baltimore, and vanishes. Discovered delirious outside polling booth on October 3, thus suggesting subsequent legend that he was dragged from poll to poll as an alcoholic "repeater." Dies October 7, ostensibly of "congestion of the brain." "The Bells" and "Annabel Lee" appear posthumously.

Contributors

HAROLD BLOOM, Sterling Professor of the Humanities at Yale University, is the author of *The Anxiety of Influence, Poetry and Repression,* and many other volumes of literary criticism. His forthcoming study, *Freud: Transference and Authority,* attempts a full-scale reading of all of Freud's major writings. A MacArthur Prize Fellow, he is general editor of five series of literary criticism published by Chelsea House. During 1987–88, he was appointed Charles Eliot Norton Professor of Poetry at Harvard University.

ROBERT L. CARRINGER is Associate Professor of English and Film Studies at the University of Illinois.

BARTON LEVI ST. ARMAND, known for his writing on Gothicism and Romanticism, including Poe and Wilde, teaches at Brown University.

WALTER STEPP is Assistant Professor of English at Nassau Community College, Garden City, New York. He has written on Henry James.

BRIAN M. BARBOUR has edited anthologies of criticism on Benjamin Franklin and on American Transcendentalism.

GREGORY S. JAY is Associate Professor of English at the University of South Carolina. He is the author of *Past and Present Voices: T. S. Eliot and the Poetry of Criticism.*

J. GERALD KENNEDY teaches at Louisiana State University. He is the author of *The Astonished Traveler: William Darby, Frontier Geographer and Man of Letters.*

KEN FRIEDEN is Assistant Professor in the Department of Modern Languages and Classics at Emory University. He is the author of *Genius and Monologue* and *The Dream of Interpretation.*

Bibliography

Auden, W. H. Introduction. In *Selected Prose and Poetry*, by Edgar Allan Poe. New York: Rinehart, 1950.

Auerbach, Jonathan. "Poe's Other Double: The Reader in the Fiction." *Criticism* 24 (1982): 341–61.

Barthes, Roland. "Textual Analysis of Poe's 'Valdemar.' " Translated by Geoff Bennington. In *Untying the Text: A Post-Structuralist Reader*, edited by Robert Young, 133–61. Boston: Routledge & Kegan Paul, 1981.

Bell, Michael Davitt. *The Development of American Romance: The Sacrifice of Relation*. Chicago: University of Chicago Press, 1980.

Benton, Richard P., ed. *New Approaches to Poe: A Symposium*. Hartford: Transcendental Books, 1970.

Bonaparte, Marie. *The Life and Works of Edgar Allan Poe*. Translated by John Rodker. London: Imago, 1949.

Brooks, Cleanth. "Edgar Allan Poe as Interior Decorator." *Ventures* 8, no. 2 (Fall 1960): 41–46.

Buranelli, Vincent. *Edgar Allan Poe*. 2d ed. Boston: Twayne, 1977.

Butler, David W. "Usher's Hypchondriasis: Mental Alienation and Romantic Idealism in Poe's Gothic Tales." *American Literature* (1976): 1–12.

Carlson, Eric W., ed. *Edgar Allan Poe: The Fall of the House of Usher*. Merrill Literary Casebook Series. Columbus: Merrill, 1971.

———, ed. *The Recognition of Edgar Allan Poe*. Ann Arbor: University of Michigan Press, 1966.

Davidson, Edward Hutchins. *Poe: A Critical Study*. Cambridge: Harvard University Press, Belknap, 1957.

Derrida, Jacques. "The Purveyor of Truth." *Yale French Studies* 52 (1976): 31–113.

Eliot, T. S. *From Poe to Valéry*. New York: Harcourt, Brace & World, 1948.

ESQ 16, suppl. (1970). Special Poe issue.

Felman, Shoshana. "On Reading Poetry: Reflections on the Limits and Possibilities of Psychoanalytical Approaches." In *The Literary Freud: Mechanisms of Defense and the Poetic Will*. New Haven: Yale University Press, 1980.

Fiedler, Leslie. *Love and Death in the American Novel*. Rev. ed. New York: Stein & Day, 1966.

Gargano, James. "The Question of Poe's Narrators." *College English* 25 (1963): 177–81.

Godden, Richard. "Edgar Poe and the Detection of Riot." *Literature and History* 8, no. 2 (1982): 206–31.

Halliburton, David. *Edgar Allan Poe: A Phenomenological Study*. Princeton: Princeton University Press, 1973.

Hirsch, David H. "The Pit and the Apocalypse." *Sewanee Review* 76 (1968): 632–52.

Hoffman, Daniel. *Poe Poe Poe Poe Poe Poe Poe*. Garden City, N.Y.: Doubleday, 1972.

Hoffman, Michael J. *The Subversive Vision: American Romanticism in Literature*. National University Publications. Port Washington, N.Y.: Kennikat, 1972.

Howarth, William, ed. *Twentieth Century Interpretations of Poe's Tales*. Englewood Cliffs, N.J.: Prentice-Hall, 1971.

Huxley, Aldous. *Music at Night and Other Essays*. London: Fountain Press, 1931.

Hyslop, Lois, and Francis E. Hyslop, Jr., eds. and trans. *Baudelaire on Poe*. State College, Pa.: Bald Eagle Press, 1952.

Irwin, John T. *American Hieroglyphics*. New Haven: Yale University Press, 1980.

Johnson, Barbara. "The Frame of Reference: Poe, Lacan, Derrida." *Yale French Studies* 55–56 (1977): 457–505.

Ketterer, David. *The Rationale of Deception in Poe*. Baton Rouge: Louisiana State University Press, 1979.

Kiely, Robert. "The Comic Masks of Edgar Allan Poe." *Umanesimo* 1, no. 5 (1967): 31–41.

Kozikowski, Stanely J. "A Reconsideration of Poe's 'The Cask of Amontillado.' " *American Transcendental Quarterly* 39 (1978): 269–80.

Lacan, Jacques. "The Seminar on 'The Purloined Letter.' " Translated by J. Mehlman. *Yale French Studies* 48 (1972).

Levin, Harry. *The Power of Blackness: Hawthorne, Poe, Melville*. New York: Knopf, 1958.

Levine, Stuart. *Edgar Poe: Seer and Craftsman*. Deland, Fl.: Everett/Edwards, 1972.

Levy, Maurice. "Poe and the Gothic Tradition." Translated by Richard Henry Harwell. *ESQ* 18, no. 1 (1972): 19–25.

Lynen, John. "The Death of the Present: Edgar Allan Poe." In *The Design of the Present: Essays on Time and Form in American Literature*. New Haven: Yale University Press, 1969.

Mankowitz, Wolf. *The Extraordinary Mr. Poe*. New York: Summit, 1978.

Moldenhauer, Joseph J. "Murder as a Fine Art: Basic Connections between Poe's Aesthetics, Psychology, and Moral Vision." *PMLA* 83 (1968): 284–97.

Pollin, Burton R. *Discoveries in Poe*. Notre Dame, Ind.: University of Notre Dame Press, 1970.

Quinn, Arthur Hobson. *Edgar Allan Poe: A Critical Biography*. New York: Appleton-Century-Crofts, 1963.

Quinn, Patrick Francis. *The French Face of Edgar Poe*. Carbondale: Southern Illinois University Press, 1957.

Regan, Robert, ed. *Poe: A Collection of Critical Essays*. Englewood Cliffs, N.J.: Prentice-Hall, 1967.

Roth, Martin. "The Poet's Purloined Letter." In *Mystery and Detection Annual 1*. Beverly Hills, Calif.: Donald Adams, 1973.

Seelye, John. "Edgar Allan Poe: *Tales of the Grotesque and Arabesque.*" In *Landmarks of American Writing,* edited by Henning Cohen, 101–10. New York: Basic Books, 1969.

Shulman, Robert. "Poe and the Powers of the Mind." *ELH* 37, no. 2 (1970): 245–62.

Smith, Alan Gardner. "Edgar Allan Poe, the Will, and Horror Fiction." In *American Fiction: New Readings,* edited by Richard Grey. Totowa, N.J.: Barnes & Noble, 1983.

———. "The Psychological Context of Three Tales by Poe." *Journal of American Studies* 7, no. 3 (1973): 279–88.

Tate, Allan. *The Forlorn Demon.* Chicago: Ayer, 1953.

Thompson, G. R. *Poe's Fiction: Romantic Irony in the Gothic Tales.* Madison: University of Wisconsin Press, 1973.

———. " 'Proper Evidence of Madness': American Gothic and the Interpretation of 'Ligeia.' " *ESQ* 18, no. 1 (1972): 30–47.

University of Mississippi Studies in English, n.s. 3 (1982). Special Poe issue.

Vanderbilt, Kermit. "Art and Nature in 'The Masque of the Red Death.' " *Nineteenth-Century Fiction* 22 (1967): 379–89.

Veler, Richard P., ed. *Papers on Poe: Essays in Honor of John Ward Ostrom.* Springfield, Ohio: Chantry Music Press, 1972.

Vitanza, Victor J. "The Question of Poe's Narrators: Perverseness Considered Once Again." *American Transcendental Quarterly* 38 (1978): 137–49.

Wilson, Edmund. *The Shores of Light.* New York: Farrar, Straus & Giroux, 1952.

Woodson, Thomas, ed. *Twentieth-Century Interpretations of "The Fall of the House of Usher."* Englewood Cliffs, N.J.: Prentice-Hall, 1969.

Zanger, Jules. "Poe and the Theme of Forbidden Knowledge." *American Literature* 49 (1978): 533–43.

———. "Poe's American Garden: 'The Domain of Arnheim.' " *American Transcendental Quarterly* 50 (1981): 93–104.

Acknowledgments

"Poe's Tales: The Circumscription of Space" (originally entitled "Circumscription of Space and the Form of Poe's *Arthur Gordon Pym*") by Robert L. Carringer from *PMLA* 89, no. 3 (May 1974), © 1974 by the Modern Language Association of America. Reprinted by permission of the Modern Language Association of America.

"The 'Mysteries' of Edgar Poe: The Quest for a Monomyth in Gothic Literature" by Barton Levi St. Armand from *The Gothic Imagination: Essays in Dark Romanticism*, edited by G. R. Thompson, © 1974 by the President and Regents of Washington State University. Reprinted by permission of Washington State University Press.

"The Ironic Double in Poe's 'The Cask of Amontillado' " by Walter Stepp from *Studies in Short Fiction* 13, no. 4 (Fall 1976), © 1977 by Newberry College. Reprinted by permission.

"Poe and Tradition" by Brian M. Barbour from *The Southern Literary Journal* 10, no. 2 (Spring 1978), © 1978 by the Department of English of the University of North Carolina at Chapel Hill. Reprinted by permission.

"Poe: Writing and the Unconscious" by Gregory S. Jay from *The American Renaissance: New Dimensions* 28, no. 1 (1983), © 1983 by Associated University Presses, Inc. Reprinted by permission.

"Phantasms of Death in Poe's Fiction" by J. Gerald Kennedy from *The Haunted Dusk: American Supernatural Fiction, 1820–1920*, edited by Howard Kerr, John W. Crowley, and Charles L. Crow, © 1983 by the University of Georgia Press. Reprinted by permission.

"Poe's Narrative Monologues" by Ken Frieden from *Genius and Monologue* by Ken Frieden, © 1985 by Cornell University. Reprinted by permission of Cornell University Press.

Index

"Purloined Letter, The" *(continued)*
doubling of the self in, 84,
100; narrator of, 66; and
nature of intelligence, 67–68;
plot-line of, 68–69; as
rejection of
Transcendentalism, 67;
revenge as theme in, 101–2;
symbolism of letter in,
100–102

Radcliffe, Ann: De Quincey on,
27; and Gothic literature, 25,
27–29, 51, 113; Keats on, 27;
and Romanticism, 28–29;
Shelley on, 27; Wordsworth
on, 28
"Rationale of Verse, The," 14
"Raven, The," 140; originality in,
98; writing of, 97–98, 99
Richardson, Samuel, first-person
narratives of, 136–39
"Rime of the Ancient Mariner,
The" (Coleridge), compared
to "The Fall of the House of
Usher," 70
Romantic literature: Blake and, 83,
86; Byron and, 88; Coleridge
and, 88; Emerson and, 86;
Manfred as, 94; Poe and, 88;
Shelley and, 88; as turning
point, 83–84; Wordsworth
and, 86, 88
Romanticism: and Gothicism,
27–28; and Gothic literature,
25–26; and human mind,
66–67; as opposed to Locke's
philosophy, 66–67; Poe's
rejection of, 83–84, 85, 86,
102; and Primitivism, 66–67;
Radcliffe and, 28–29; ruins
and tradition of, 36–37; and
suicide, 122

St. Aubert, Emily de (*Mysteries of
Udolpho*), as Gothic character,
27–28

Scientific rationalism, "The
Purloined Letter" as criticism
of, 69
Sexuality: in "Morella," 91; in
Poe's short stories, 22, 84,
108–9; in "The Murders in the
Rue Morgue," 99
"Shadow—A Parable," death
motif in, 118–19
Shamela (Fielding), as parody of
Pamela, 138–39
Shelley, Percy: on Ann Radcliffe,
27; and Romantic literature,
88
"Sleeper, The," 140
"Sonnet—Silence," 121
"Sonnet—To Science," 67
Sorrows of Young Werther (Goethe),
122
Soul, the: and death, 114–15,
127–28; physiological
existence of, 127–29
Southern literary tradition, and
Poe, 12
Spence, Lewis, on Egyptian
mysteries, 41, 43
Suicide: of Chatterton, 122; in
Poe's stories, 122–24;
Romanticism and, 122; and
Sorrows of Young Werther, 122
Supernaturalism: and Gothic
literature, 112–13; motifs of,
111–12, 113–14
Swedenborg, Emanuel, and occult
mysteries, 42–43

Tales of the Grotesque and Arabesque,
112
"Tamerlane," 84, 140
"Tell-Tale Heart, The," 17, 22;
compulsion in, 122; delimiting
of space as motif in, 23;
doubling of the self in, 84;
narrator of, 140–41, 143;
psychological realism in,
140–41